I met Dr. Gerald Young in 1989 through my late husband, Dr. E. Thurman Walker, Jr. Dr. Young and Dr. Walker shared a unique bond that transcended time and distance. They learned and grew together as fellow seminary students, preachers, pastors, and brothers.

As a result, I have been blessed to observe the evolution of the Rev. Dr. G. Martin Young as he has become a prolific and persuasive "voice" through the past two decades. Dr. Young has consistently challenged his readers and congregations as he has shared the importance of a real and relevant relationship with God.

Insanity of Theology: God-Talkers Dressed with Inner Vestments is a masterpiece. In it Dr. Young lays out the process for experiencing a working knowledge with God, belief in the Christ, encountering the work of the Spirit, and embracing a life-changing and authentic church environment. This is truly a book to be shared and utilized not only by church leaders, but anyone who seeks a more sincere and genuine spiritual life.

Jo Angelia Simpson
Founder, Palm Tree Woman Project™

Dr. Young's book, *Insanity of Theology,* is a unique book that strives to publicly and practically apply the rigors of theological inquiry to the stress and strain of life's twists and turns. Focusing on Theology Proper, Christology, Pneumatology, and Ecclesiology, Young presents a vibrant picture of a lived-out theology in the face of a tarnished experience. Young believes that trusting in God takes an applicable theology. Rooted in the doctrine of the Church, Young provides a cultural apologetic to the strains of our life by using pop culture and various avenues across generations to present a message that reiterates that unless you are able to live out and live in the beliefs that you have you are living in vain.

Dr. Dante D. Wright I
Senior Pastor of Sweet Home – The Pinnacle of Praise, Round Rock, Texas

Rev. Dr. G. Martin Young is a venerable giant among preachers, enlightening us over the years and enhancing the knowledge of readers and seminarians throughout this nation. I strongly recommend *Insanity of Theology* to Bible students and those who mentor them across this country. I would recommend that every believer read this book! In reading it, you will find a gold mine of information that will assist you in every aspect of your ministry. Dr. Young has the gift of making complex concepts accessible to every reader. In this powerful book, he vividly expresses how his experiences underlined his beliefs and faith. He takes his readers on a spiritual journey by giving them five classes of what he defines as "God-Talkers." I want to say to Dr. G. Martin Young, thank you for this book. You unashamedly challenge readers to integrity, perseverance, character, and ultimately to faith in the Lord Jesus Christ.

Rev. Edmund T. Sherrill, M.Ed.
Mt. Enon Baptist Church, Philadelphia, Pennsylvania

Dr. G. Martin Young's *Insanity of Theology* is an outstanding contribution to Christian thought. It was birthed in personal tribulation and written during deep contemplation in a manner that makes it contemporary in application and elevating in spirit. Young's work transcends traditional theological books by providing a deeply fulfilling intellectual and spiritual experience. I heartily recommend this outstanding gift to the Church.

Edward L. Taylor, PhD.
Royal Holloway, University of London, The United Kingdom,
President/CEO Taylor Ministries,
Editor, *The Words of Gardner Taylor* Series

I love what Dr. G. Martin Young is doing in *Insanity of Theology*. He has made a bold move in taking the discussion of Theology from the Halls of Higher Learning and bringing Theology to the marketplaces of everyday life. He brings together Theology, God-Talkers, and Inner Vestments as key components in overcoming any adversity life brings our way by using good insanity that brings positive change and post-traumatic growth. This book is refreshing, inspiring, uplifting, and life-changing. I recommend it highly.

Bishop C. E. Glover
Senior Pastor of Mt Bethel Ministries, Ft. Lauderdale, Florida

Dr. G. Martin Young has done it again! He is on the divine cutting edge of proper and popular theological thought, as shares his accurate and effective knowledge of the scriptures. He gives us Christian reading that is comfortable to the practical and yet profound to those who need a crisp and challenging thought to support these times. I say to those of you in Christian Book Land, relax, read, and rejoice in what the Holy Spirit has laid on Dr. Young's heart to give to us in these crucial times.

Rev. Zachary Lee, Sr.
Mt. Paran Baptist Church, Moderator of the New Salem District,
Second Vice-President St. Louis Minister's Union,
Fourth Vice-President Baptist General State Congress,
Special Assistant to the National Baptist Congress President, E. St. Louis, Illinois

In *Insanity of Theology*, Dr. G. Martin Young exposed himself to the reader by sharing his story of how the Lord brought him out of the darkest valley period of his life. During this challenging time, Dr. Young learned the ability to look deep into his inner self in order to uncover the importance of Inner Vestments. Now eight years later, the Lord has ushered Dr. Young into a new dimension of living out his divine purpose. I encourage you to allow the words in this book to encourage a self-inventory to search for the Inner Vestments in your life. Once you find these Inner Vestments then use these tools to speak life into others who are experiencing the vicissitudes of life.

Rev. Justin M. Shamell, M. Div.
Atlanta, Georgia

Dr. G. Martin Young continues to challenge our thinking about what we see in the world. He is a seasoned author and administrator in theological education; here again, he has taken the "Why not" and given to us "Why." This new entry into Dr. Young's journey of writing what is on his mind is a solid contribution to today's Church.

Dr. Elliot Cuff
Pastor, Lincoln Heights Missionary Baptist Church
Dean of National Baptist Congress

Dr. G. Martin Young captures the essence of the believer's struggle to cope with what appears to be the absence of God as the believer contends with the challenges of life. We like Job struggle with the question of God's awareness and concern about what we are going through at these times because we cannot detect God's presence. We find ourselves asking the question, "Where are you, Lord"? Our faith and witness gain strength and affirmation when we persevere through these periods of trial and test.

James A. Gibson, Jr.
Senior Pastor, Greater Temple Missionary Baptist Church, Birmingham, Alabama

Insanity of Theology by Dr. G. Martin Young is a provocative exposition that approaches our understanding of theology through a different contemporary lens. It is a must-read for pastors, seminarians, and church leaders. It is profound yet practical and will help one's understanding of the challenges faced by the 21st century Church.

Dr. Brett Snowden
Pastor, True Faith Inspirational Baptist Church,
Associate Dean, National Baptist Congress, Tampa, Florida

It is my great pleasure to congratulate Dr. G. Martin Young on his eighth book, *Insanity of Theology*. This work intertwines scholarship, pop culture, Black Church flavor, as well as personal testimony to speak to the kind of spiritual vestments that we must wear in order to continue to grow spiritually, overcome adversity, and live victoriously to the glory of God. Is theology truly insane? Read and see!

Pastor Cecilia L. Clemons
Renton First UMC, Renton, Washington

My longtime colleague and friend has done it again and even better with this new and 8th book titled *Insanity of Theology: God-Talkers Dressed with Inner Vestments*. Dr. Young proves it's not what happens to you externally; it's in your inner person that is renewed daily during those crucibles. *Insanity of Theology* is written personably, with precision, poise and purpose. Read it and receive a revelation. Thank you, Dr. G. M. Young.

Pastor Cedric Malone
Greater Mount Zion Baptist Church, Roanoke, Virginia

My friend and brother, Dr. G. Martin Young continues his rise as the Phoenix from the depth of his personal struggles and experiences. He has not only learned about God but has grown spiritually and developed wisdom. He has written a thought-provoking theological treatise to address the malaise of our current generation. Dr. Young has brought to written expression the importance of theological reflection, God-talk, and the wearing of Inner Vestments of authentic Christianity to anchor one's faith and emerge victorious from the downward spiral of hopelessness, depression, and despair. He demonstrates that faith in God is a trustworthy foundation to begin a fresh start and that hope is truly an anchor for the soul. This book is a must-read for such a time as this.

Dr. Edward O. Williamson
Pastor-teacher, Bethel Baptist Church, White Plains, New York,
Northeast Regional Coordinator SSPB-DCEAC

Dr. G. Martin Young, a proven theologian, academician, pastor, and pulpiteer, now puts pen to paper and shares wonderful insights that challenge the reader to move to a higher level of living. In this exciting, thought-provoking, and heart-probing reading, we are challenged to rid ourselves of our attachment to the look of our outer vestments, and then to invest in the content of our Inner Vestments. While "God-Talker's" priority has been on giving attention to the outer vestments that we wear to impress others in hope that they may find value in us, the author encourages us to make our priority the attention we give to our Inner Vestments, which is indicative of our relationship with the Lord and how we value Him. Dr. Young brilliantly shows the reader that there is a higher level of living that we can obtain when our hearts, souls, and minds model that of the Lord and we begin to not "looketh on the outward appearance, but … looketh on the heart" (1 Sam. 16:7).

Rev. Dr. Augustus T. Curry, Esq.
Pastor, Cornerstone Church, Fayetteville, Georgia

Dr. G. Martin Young challenges the reader to assess their inner vestments and to adorn oneself with cautious care so that your outward appearance does not overshadow the source and substance of your faith. *Insanity of Theology* is an intriguing adventure into the world of theology, pointing us to a visible God in the movies, books, and on stage. The God of our talk is walking among us and if we look closely and incline our ears to hear, we will see Him and hear His voice.

Pastor Delores J. Cain
Heritage Christian Community Baptist Church, Tampa, Florida

Dr. G. Martin Young takes us on a journey. At times the road is straight. At times our thoughts are challenged but immediately put at ease. *Insanity of Theology* is not for the occasional pursuit of God. In this powerful theological un-redacted book, Dr. Young invites all whose belief and faith is in fierce pursuit of God! Dr. Young positions God-Talkers to think theology, do theology, and live theology and theologians to rethink theology in terms of its ultimate aim, which is God!

I thoroughly appreciate how G. Martin provides a word of sense and direction to those whose hearts, souls, and minds have been captivated by the theological perspective of religious fanaticism and religious pluralism. *Insanity of Theology* clarifies and distinguishes its purpose that does not seek to explain itself, nor does it seek to apologize for any inconvenience, but violates culture, established systems, kingdoms, and governments when the message of a Sane God is to be proclaimed. For the love of God transcends culture. He pursues in order to engage humankind…we in turn seek to understand it. How insane?

Dr. Joe Stevenson
Senior Pastor, Macedonia New Life Church
Director of Continuing Education & Associate Professor of Pastoral Care,
Shaw University School of Divinity, Raleigh, North Carolina

Dr. G. Martin Young's book, *Insanity of Theology*, compels persons who delight in "God Talk" to acknowledge the insanity of continuing to believe and have faith in God to turn situations around for the better, despite the circumstances. Young, motivated by a personal journey that was once filled with the darkest and most painful moments of his life, speaks to the only constant that kept him – his theology. In this work, Young approaches his central theme that declares that to the rest of the world that it is insane to continue to affirm the reputation of God for outcomes to life's painful and devastating circumstances, but his approach is fresh as he invites the voices of theologians from halls of academia, protagonists from leading movies, and social commentators from contemporary pop culture to weigh in. This is a thought-provoking work that will challenge the reader to search deeply to reignite the fire in mind, body, and soul to continue to hold to a faith in God that will sustain and reveal.

Vanessa Oliver Ward
Lecturer, Old Testament, United Theological Seminary,
Co-Pastor, Omega Baptist Church, Dayton, Ohio

Insanity of Theology is an instructive look at the challenges of walking by faith, depending on God, and trusting that the outcomes of our journey are working for our good. Dr. Young shares personal stories of redemption and victory through difficulty because of an "Insane Theology."

Pastor Thomas Fisher
Second Baptist Church, Redwood City, California

Dr. G. Martin Young is a recent acquaintance of mine and a co-worker at the Seminary, and I've always delighted in his humor. But through his writings, I have come to admire his thought processes tremendously. In reading his book, *Insanity of Theology*, I came to a deepening knowledge and understanding of him, not only as a person of deep faith, but also as a pastor/mentor/writer. His keen mind has zeroed in on what life can be like as a Christian immersed in the Spirit, while at the same time acknowledging pain and grief, even times bordering on unbelief. Young has come through such trials and has created a thought-provoking book to help all of us come to and through our own pain, encouraging our own faith to stay deep-rooted, helping us to rely on the mighty support system found in the Trinity, which to those who do not know Christ, sounds insane! An easy read, you will find much comfort and help in this book.

Janice Kronour
United Theological Seminary, Dayton, Ohio

In a very real and practical way, Dr. G. Martin Young has bridged the gap from theory to practice. He has systematically demonstrated how to walk authentically with the Lord solely based on His principles and precepts despite circumstances, world systems, or challenges we may face. Dr. Young encourages a transparency in living our lives to be aligned, personally and collectively, with the truths of who God is! Through *Insanity of Theology*, we are inspired to examine Scripture as God intended and, in turn, live transformed lives consistent with a faith that delineates who God is!

Patrice L. Pye, Ph.D.
Clinical Psychologist
Member, Cornerstone Christian Church, Shiloh, Illinois

We're always talking about God and encountering Him in all the experiences of our lives whether we realize it or not. While we do not think of ourselves as theologians in the classical sense, Dr. G. Martin Young has shown us, based upon his own personal experience, how we can experience God in the negative times of our lives to help strengthen our relationship with Him, deepen our faith in Him, and be clearer in terms of what we believe and do not believe about Him. This concrete experience with God is what gives us character, or what Young calls being dressed with Inner Vestments. *Insanity of Theology* is a book every person ought to read in order to take their understanding of God out of some nebulous philosophical category and allow Him to be real as He walks with us through the day-to-day experiences of our lives.

Get this book today! You will be blessed!

James Perkins
Senior Pastor, Greater Christ Baptist Church, Author, and
20th President of the Progressive National Baptist Convention, Inc.

Charles Gerkin notes in *The Living Human Document*, "every person's life is like a novel or a book to be read." Dr. Gerald Young has laid his life before us. We read with intrigue his lack, his pain, and his sorrows that are complimented by God's provision, God's presence, and God's peace. We leave with an assurance about God.

Pastor Caroles S. Taylor
Friendship Baptist Church, Columbia, Missouri

GOD-TALKERS DRESSED WITH INNER VESTMENTS

INSANITY
of Sheology

DR. G. MARTIN YOUNG
FOREWORD BY DR. CHARLES E. BOOTH

MMGI BOOKS • CHICAGO

Published by MMGI Books, Chicago, IL 60636
www.mmgibooks.com

Insanity of Theology: God-Talkers Dressed with Inner Vestments
Copyright © 2014 by G. Martin Young, Dayton, Ohio 45406

All rights reserved. Except for brief quotations used in reviews, articles, or other media, no part of this book may be reproduced or transmitted in any form or by any means, electronic or mechanical, including photocopying, recording, or by information storage or retrieval system, without permission by the publisher.

Except for quotations from Scripture, the quoted ideas expressed in the book are not, in all cases, exact quotations, as some have been edited for clarity and brevity. In all cases, the author has attempted to maintain the speaker's original intent. In some cases, quoted material for this book was obtained from secondary sources, primarily print media. While every effort was made to ensure the accuracy of these sources, the accuracy cannot be guaranteed.

Library of congress Cataloging-in-Publication Data

Insanity of Theology: God-Talkers Dressed with Inner Vestments

G. Martin Young

p. cm

ISBN 978-1-4951-1240-9 (pbk. :alk. Paper)

Religious life. 2. Conduct of life. 3. Christian Education.

Young, G. Martin

Printed in the U.S.A.

All Scripture quotations are taken from the Message. Copyright © Eugene H. Peterson 1993, 1994, 1995. Used by permission ofNavPress Publishing Group.

To Dr. Harold Hudson

The Ancient Celtic tradition of *Anam Cara* recognizes that connecting with another person is "becoming open and trusting with that individual—inclusive of two souls flowing together." If such a union is formed, in the tradition of *Anam Cara*, one has found a "Soul Friend." Dr. Harold Hudson, I am honored for your mentoring, and I am truly blessed to have you as a "Soul Friend." And tell your gorgeous wife, Billie, I praise God for her, too!!!

But regarding anything beyond this, dear friend, go easy. There's no end to the publishing of books, and constant study wears you out so you're no good for anything else. The last and final word is this:

Fear God.

Do what he tells you.

Ecclesiastes 12:12, 13

Words of Special Thanks

Endeavors would not have been possible without the unconditional love of my Proverbs 31 wife, Muriel. Your commitment to what God has placed inside of me has allowed me to pursue God's perfect will for my life and ministry. Thank you for your prayers and unwavering support, which have never had occasion to fail me.

Thank you to the plethora of men and women of God who have deposited richly into my life—including:

- My best friend, the Reverend Donald Robinson (my elder brother), his mother, Elder Jane Irene Shelton Robinson, and his lovely wife, Kristi. He is the Senior Pastor of the Marine Baptist Church of New Orleans, Louisiana.
- My best friend, the Reverend Dr. Kerwin "Big Thunder" Lee, and his gorgeous wife, Yolanda (I love you all dearly) of the Berean Christian Church of Stone Mountain, Georgia.
- Bishop Broderick Huggins and his gorgeous wife, Toni, Senior Pastor of the B.A. Huggins Ministries and Senior Pastor of the St. Paul Baptist Church, Oxnard, California.
- Reverend T. Ellsworth Gant, II and his lovely wife, Tofa, Senior Pastor of the Second Baptist Church of Riverside, California.
- Reverend L. E. Campbell, Senior Pastor of Park Avenue Missionary Baptist Church of Riverside, California.
- Reverend Dwight Jones and his great wife, Sandra, Senior Pastor of Crown of Life Ministries of Riverside, California.
- Senior Pastor LaTerra Ruffin of Moreno Valley, California.

In your own way, each of you has encouraged me to stay the course and remain committed to the cause of our Christ. I also offer the fondest appreciation to the Reverend Dr. Christopher Davis of the St. Paul Baptist Church of Memphis, Tennessee and my great friend, The Rev. Clanton C.W. Dawson, Jr., PhD., of Columbia, Missouri. Your unending support has provided me with constant leaning posts. Special thanks to the formidable Mr. Chris Gardner of Chicago, Illinois, from the 2006 film *The Pursuit of Happyness*. I also extend sincere thanks to my eternal friend, Patricia Casey; my sister in Christ and my special friend in the Lord, Jane Jelks Jones; her husband, Deacon Earl Jones, and her preaching son (my brother), Kenyatta Jelks, Pastor of the Mt. Tabor Baptist Church of Columbus, Georgia; and my Dean, Dr. Edward Wheeler of Jacksonville, Florida. Thank you all for being a blessing.

Forever in God's Service,

Dr. G. Martin Young

Contents

Foreword 1

Prolegomenon 3

Prologue 11

Chapter 1

The God Who Writes Straight on Crooked Lined Paper

THE INNER VESTMENT OF GOD 27
"The quest to implement more knowledge of God into one's personal life"

The God-Talker's Knowledge of God 34
"He can pull you out of the darkest of night"

The Indiana Jones and the Last Crusade Knowledge of God 38
"Passing the tests to get closer to God"

The Avatar Ian's Knowledge of God 41
"Going beyond cloaked garments of religion"

The 12 Years a Slave Knowledge of God 44
"We're not exempt but not alone either"

The Book of Eli Knowledge of God 47
"Take the Word on your journey"

The 47 Ronin Knowledge of God 50
"Devotion to our King"

God-Talker's Golden Rule 53
"Living life like it's golden"

Chapter 2
The Savior Who Travels Down Dead-End Streets

THE INNER VESTMENT OF CHRIST 59
"The journey to be more like Him in a devalued world"

The God-Talker's Remix Version of Belief in Christ 65
"Out of the picture frame and into the world"

700 Left-Handed Believers in Christ 71
"Being left-handed is a good thing"

Clear the Air Belief in Christ 76
"Justice is color-blind"

Impossible Odds Belief in Christ 80
"Can't count us out"

God-Talker's Anthem 84
"'Tis so sweet"

Chapter 3
The Spirit That Aids Drunks Walking Tightrope Wires

THE INNER VESTMENT OF THE HOLY SPIRIT 89
"The mission of Heaven's Global Positioning System is to keep us balanced and on course"

The God-Talker Empowered by the Spirit 94
"The flow"

The Side Effects of Being Empowered by the Spirit 101
"We want His side effects"

The Spiritual Kintsukurio Process of Being Empowered by the Spirit 108
"Lord, remake us"

The Spiritual Kaizen Experience of Being Empowered by the Spirit 117
"Afraid of change no longer"

God-Talker's Mantra 123
"Keep the Flame burning bright"

CHAPTER 4

The Church That Gathers Down by the Riverside

THE INNER VESTMENT OF THE AUTHENTIC CHURCH 127
"The pursuit of the House of Heaven is to be clothed in Blood-washed garments"

The God-Talker's Encounter with the Authentic Church 137
"On the move"

5,000 Men and Women on 500 Corners Encounter the Authentic Church 143
"The things God cannot do"

On Behalf of the Called-Out Ones' Encounter with the Authentic Church 149
"Our Personal Benefactor"

God-Talker's Mission 154
"Not lying on the Trinity"

Conclusion 159

Glossary 161

Notes 165

Foreword

Whether we realize it or not all who believe in God are theologians of some sort. We may not be systematic in our theological assertions; however, whenever we talk about God or express opinions about His being, actuality, and involvement in the human experience, we are articulating a theological perspective. Perhaps the best way to succinctly declare what I am trying to say is to suggest that believers are practical theologians in that we are always seeking to formulate from a rational perspective our understanding of God. To those who are non-believers, and believers are guilty as well, there are times when the Almighty escapes all reason and, seemingly, makes no sense at all. Regardless of the nomenclature we attach to God—Jehovah, Yahweh, Elohim, Adonai, El-Shaddai—there are times when God makes absolutely no sense at all. This is by no means a statement of sacrilege. In fact, that lyrical prophetic genius of the Old Testament, Isaiah, speaks for all of Him when he says—

"I don't think the way you think.
The way you work isn't the way I work."
God's Decree.
"For as the sky soars high above earth,
so the way I work surpasses the way you work,
and the way I think is beyond the way you think." (Isaiah 55:8-9)

While the actions of God often elude us, we must rejoice that God is always approachable. It is with these thoughts that Dr. G. Martin Young has undertaken the arduous task of inviting us into a "creative encounter" with the One who opens Himself to human scrutiny and question. Dr. Young invites us to explore *Insanity of Theology*.

I commend the reader of this unique work to appreciate and carefully think through the unique way in which the author uses contemporary movies as metaphors in our quest to seek understanding of the One who, more often than not, remains elusive—so near, yet, so far away.

I am convinced that Dr. Young is on to something when he summons us to think about God in ways that are before us daily and, yet, we have the tendency to not hear His voice, see His activity and grasp the message He is seeking to convey. The author forces us to see God not only in cinema, but also in the critical crucibles of life's daily drama.

In reading *Insanity of Theology* one is liberated in one's confrontation with the Eternal. The beauty of God is that He welcomes our scrutiny and is not offended by our quest to draw closer to Him. This work is a welcomed volume because we are challenged to think critically about this awesome God we confess and profess. Perhaps as you prayerfully leaf your way through this book you will arrive at its conclusion with the thought that my belief system has been theologically enlightened and my discipleship deepened.

Dr. Charles E. Booth, Senior Pastor
Mt. Olivet Baptist Church
Columbus, Ohio

Prolegomenon

Just as the Gospel of Luke continues in Acts of the Apostles, this book is a continuation of experience from my fifth book, *Surviving Category 5 Heartaches*. If you haven't read this book, it summarizes my fall after divorce, and how I struggled for eight or nine years to rebuild my life. It was extremely painful, nerve-racking, heart-breaking, and filled with tears and sleepless nights. On a scale of 1–10, I would rate myself a negative 5.

I found myself homeless and living out of a 1993 Honda for some seven or eight months, and lodging at a Motel 6 or similar housing, while fighting off suicidal thoughts and existing on welfare. Then, one morning, after awaking in the midst of darkness from a sleepless night, I blinked and realized I had lost eight years of my life. I learned a lot in the dark, including the desire to be transparent—to share my story with others, and help them on their journey through life's devastating times.

This book is a continuation in the sense that it chronicles the three things I learned from those eight years of darkness, things that have been the constant threads that held me together for over 30 years of preaching the Gospel of Jesus Christ.

The first constant thread is my theology—what I believe about God. This thread is based upon what I experienced from my relationship with God, and what I have learned about Him. In fact, what I learned was the *Insanity of Theology*. The second constant thread taught me that as a God-Talker, you must be consistent so that what you say lines up to what you really believe. I learned to be a stronger God-Talker. The third constant thread gave me insights of our

Inner Vestments—our clothing that identifies true religion. This insight was invaluable in teaching me the importance of Inner Vestments.

It is these three threads that have closed the curtain of night and opened the curtain of day. It is these three threads that have made a world of difference and breathed in me new life, moving me from a negative 5 to a positive 8. It is these three threads that have gotten me back on my feet, made me more determined to keep running this race, and proven to me that post-traumatic growth is possible and best when magnified. Post-traumatic growth is growing spiritually even after each episode of heartache and pain. Post-traumatic growth is gained after looking deep inside oneself and being honest with the person whom you find. Post-traumatic growth is crucial to moving into a solid relationship with Heaven; where rather than being bitter from your storms, you are made better because of them. Post-traumatic growth or benefit-finding refers to positive psychological change experienced as a result of the struggle with highly challenging life circumstances. The highly challenging life circumstances really promoted growth in my thinking, belief, and conversations about God. The purpose of this book is to present these three threads in moving, creative, and poignant ways.

First, there is Theology. Each day I would get up and say today is the day God will bless me to get a job, a place to live, a car, and a church to pastor, and so on. This is good insanity. I woke up one morning after eight years of darkness and said to myself, "What I'm doing is insane," according to the world's definition. But this is good insanity. I'm doing the same thing over and over expecting God to give me a different result. I was surviving with barely enough to eat; not having bus fare; and no money to pay for the next night's place to sleep. These images gave birth to the name "*Insanity of Theology*." For me, this is a good insanity.

The underlying premise to this book is to acknowledge the thoughts of many: that faith in God is insane! In reality, the truly insane are those who think that they can have a fulfilling life without faith in God. To some it is insanity to have faith in the face of what appears to be surely a hopeless situation. To some it is insanity to have faith when everything that you've had of seeming worth is gone. To some it is insanity to have faith when you don't have a pot to potty, or a window to discard the human waste. To some it is insanity to believe in something or a force greater than you, when it doesn't seem like that force is doing anything to help you out of your current situation or set of circumstances.

But to those suffering from these destructive perceptions, I say that true insanity is in not believing in the God who created the heavens and the earth. To those I say true insanity is in not believing in the God who caused the Red Sea to stand up in salute to the heavens and allow the children of Israel to walk through to the other side on dry land. To those I say true insanity is refusing to believe in the God who kept Shadrach, Meshach, and Abednego from being consumed by fire in the fiery furnace even though it was turned up three times hotter than normal, and allowed them to walk out unsinged and unharmed. To those I say true insanity is refusing to believe in the God who stood between the woman caught in adultery and her accusers, who saved her life and gave her a new start. To all who face challenges, we can't afford to not believe in God regardless of what the world says. To the contrary, although there are limits to what we can do, there are no limits to what God can do.

Secondly, consider the God-Talkers. This book will help us to understand more about the audacious faith that never disappoints; to think together about the kind of intentional "God-Talk" that will keep us growing as individuals, families, congregations, and communities. We need to become God-Talkers and share with others about this God, and explore together more about our God. Through the years, my grip in the gospel has become wiser and stronger. As I stepped in from the cold and indifferent world, I was drawn closer to God; and through the work of the Holy Spirit, His word provided the warmth for my mind, heart, and soul.

The good news from God is that a bridge can be built that will connect God's Word to our mind, heart, and soul, returning us to the cross; and will bless our walk with Him. God's Word renews, rebuilds, regenerates, and revives us to the extent that there will be growth and maturity in spite of adversity. Through the years, I have become "real" in the Body of Christ. We must admit that we have not always been saved and sanctified; that we have real problems, real issues, and real human feelings. We are not mannequin Christians but individuals who have struggles that only God can handle. We must live what we believe, and fight every day to have that life that God has promised we might have, even in this world—*life more abundantly*.

Over the years and especially over the past nine years I stayed in the fight! God's Word can make a difference in our lives. His Word says that we are overcomers, not quitters, not losers, not defeatists. So then, when we stray away from the flame of God, ask for forgiveness. Ask God to help us stand on His promise that even in the face of spiritual lapses, we can still be a Church after His own heart. And, when we slip into these momentary failures, and we will, we must strive to move quickly to correct our slothfulness in answering God's call.

Over the years and especially over the past nine years I ask daily, "God, please fill us with Your presence daily." Believers require a continuous filling of communion with God day-by-day, moment-by-moment, and with each second, so that He may influence, guide, and lead us in our daily walk. We are dependent upon Him to provide the wind for our sails, that we may become more like Christ. Let us make no mistake about this: our passion for God requires daily attention, consistent work, and, most of all, an obedient spirit.

Thirdly, there are Inner Vestments. This book will help us dress with the garments of wisdom and thoughts that will keep us warm in the chill of night. We must robe with Inner Vestments that keep our hearts, minds, and souls in Christ Jesus so that we can continue to grow in faithfulness, wisdom, witness, and victory! We robe with Inner Vestments that will feed our desire to be clothed for victorious living, loving, and leveraging for the Kingdom of God. We robe in inner vestments that are "Special Delivered" straight from the heavenly tailor shop that fit us with what we need to weather any storms, challenges, situations, and heartaches. These vestments provide knowledge that sets the captive free; belief that gives reason to be a worshipper; power to drop chains of bondage; and encounters that leave onlookers in AWE. When we put on heaven's clothes, God becomes omnipresent—the "Lord is truly everywhere." King David expressed this great news:

> Is there anyplace I can go to avoid your Spirit? To be out of your sight? If I could climb to the sky, you're there! If I go underground, you're there! If I flew on morning's wings to the far western horizon, You'd find me in a minute—You're already there waiting! Then I said to myself, "Oh, He even sees me in the dark! At night I'm immersed in the light!"
> (Psalm 139:7-10)

As long as we are dressed in His robe, we can never escape His glorious presence.

As a customer of "Heaven Tailors," you will find answers to questions that have been asked from the beginning of time; and that answer will remain the same throughout eternity: "No, there is nothing too hard for God." He has a multiplicity of resources far beyond human comprehension or imagination, for His ways are far beyond the bounds of human research. Consider 2 Kings 19:35 where God sends His angels into the camps and all the men are rendered dead. Consider 2 Chronicles 20:23 when God turns brothers in arms to go against one another. Look at 1 Samuel 14 where God allows Jonathan and his armor bearer to gain victory over the multitude, or at 2 Kings 7 when the four lepers experience God's turning up the volume on the army of the Syrians.

Clearly, it does not matter if the situation or circumstance is earthly calamity or spiritual peril, believers can still sing a song of victory just as Moses did, declaring that God is involved in human affairs. Inner Vestments unveil a God who is involved in human affairs. Further, His clothes bring to the situation The

Lamb that denotes the presence of God in spiritual affairs. God is an army of one! Just as He leapt over mountains, scaled the skies, and crossed the valleys during biblical days, He speaks to our difficulties and challenges, moves barriers, and performs miracles in our lives even today. His clothes speak through songs of illustrations, His clothes give illumination, and His clothes are full of the Spirit that provides inspiration.

God reveals to us the thread that is woven together and makes up these Inner Vestments. The thread is His voice. The voice of God is louder still than any of the trials of life. His voice continues to speak with love and power that penetrates through present-day barriers we believers face today. God moves with agile grace and rapid speed for the sole purpose of providing restoration to those whom He loves to wholeness in every circumstance according to His heart's desire for the people of God. The faithful Church listens with grateful anticipation for God's arrival, knowing that His presence changes all situations (2 Samuel 22:30).

The underlining theme of this book, *Insanity of Theology* (a good insanity), declares that Inner Vestments for God-Talkers are not only needed, but are given freely and are required to be worn in everyday life. You are invited to wear these extraordinary threads for this present age in need of extraordinary guidance.

John's Gospel provides evidence that leads one to conclude that the Trinity and the Authentic Church desire to reach out and stretch creation in the area of Theology, to meet humankind where they are and move them to places and spaces they would love for us to be, hoping that humankind will grapple with their understanding and grow from such an encounter, and be better off from said struggle. Insanity of Theology (which promotes an ongoing belief and faith in God to turn situations around for the betterment of the individual, the Church, and the community, even when the evidence points to the impossible), God-Talkers—the class one must pass through, and Inner Vestments—garments worn on the inside of human beings, are present to aid humankind toward winning against the powerlessness of religion that is cloaked in outer garments instead of the power that comes from their proper usage. It is through their power that life can be worth living despite sorrows, burdens, lamenting situations, and unhappiness. Keep the faith and things will change for the best. Invitations have been sent to the breadth, length, and width of the universe. Accept the invitation from John 3:16 and join others at the table.

Prologue

It was after midnight at the kitchen table while I was eating a peanut butter and jelly sandwich and drinking some apple-flavored "Juicy Juice" that a wrestling match was underway. It was between the lifelong contender "The Interrogator" and me. His interrogation was concerning my definition of *Insanity of Theology*, which I gleaned from studying the Gospel of John. What makes my definition of theology insane stems from my ongoing belief and faith in God to turn situations around for the betterment of the individual, the Church, and the community, even when the evidence points to the impossible. It is insane, says "The Interrogator," for people to keep on doing the same thing over and over again, with the expectation of a different outcome because of God. Down through the ages, the argument of "The Interrogator" has remained the same—that while it makes no good sense to keep doing the same thing over and over the outcome will not change even if God is in the equation. Sitting at the table with me and "The Interrogator" are the other three participants in this wrestling match:

- I sat in chair number 1 with my definition of *Insanity of Theology* that is taken from the Gospel of John.
- To my right, in chair number 2, were the three burning questions from Dr. Jacquelyn Grant, Professor of Systematic Theology at the Interdenominational Theological Center (ITC) in Atlanta, Georgia.
- In chair number 3 to my left was Dr. Howard Thurman's book *The Creative Encounter*.
- In chair number 4 to his left were my thoughts on "Inner Vestments."
- And, in chair number 5, directly in front of me, sat "The Interrogator."

Again, in chair number 1 is my definition of *Insanity of Theology*—promotes an ongoing belief and faith in God to turn situations around for the betterment of the individual, the Church, and the community, even when the evidence points to the impossible. My definition is under attack by "The Interrogator," who works for Satan. This force is constantly bombarding me with darts of doubt, arrows of indecision, and rocks of condemnation, and it moves directed toward hurting, crippling, and breaking me in the worst kind of ways. It was a wrestling match between my being good, as represented in the first four chairs, versus my being defeated by Evil, as represented in the fifth chair. If I lose, my survival, my good works, and my faith in the Almighty as a born-again Christian will end. If I win, my demise by the ruler of Darkness surely will not happen. So I keep wrestling and hoping for the best. He is a formidable opponent and I fight off his assaults using every ounce of strength. In my hour of need, I call for Heaven's agents, tools, and instruments to join with me in this wrestling match and revitalize my inner belief and faith in God. With each passing second, minute, and hour the first four chairs step up their game, which provides the invigoration needed to win against Satan and his interrogator.

In chair number 2, the three questions from Dr. Grant's class are pronounced:

1) What does theology really say?
2) What does theology really mean?
3) What does God want displayed in our theological lives?

It was the experience of this class that underlined my belief and faith, my theology, and the birth of a new term that now defines me, whereby, I viewed myself using the term "God-Talker," and to be more exact, a Christian God-Talker. This class was essential in my becoming a positive God-Talker. What then is a positive Christian God-Talker? In my definition, a positive Christian God-Talker has several descriptions: a fan and follower of the Christ; a believer in the Most High; a walker of faith; a water walker; a witness of God; a Christian (Christ-like); an imitator of Jesus; a sinner saved by grace; a person who has gone by Calvary and received forgiveness of sin and stopped by Pentecost and been endowed with the power to walk right and talk right; a person after God's own heart; a prisoner of hope; an accepter of the Holy Spirit; a claimer of the Body of Christ; one who believes in miracles, signs, and wonders; and one who is a friend of God. All of these characteristics define a God-Talker. In essence, a God-Talker is one whose belief and faith compel a continual grasping for understanding of Him. I am a positive Christian God-Talker. Furthermore, it is my belief that God-Talkers consist of five classes:

- *Provincial "God-Talkers."* These are persons who engage in God-Talk occasionally, like Lil Wayne, 2 Chainz, Rick Ross, guys on the corner and persons in barber or beauty shops, actors or actresses who play a religious role, secular singers who sing gospel, and the list goes on and on.
- *Practical "God-Talkers."* These persons engage in talking about God seriously and on an everyday basis. However, their talk may be positive or negative. Positive "God-Talkers" engage in theological discussions at church, community, home, work, places they frequent, and small groups where they speak positive acts and actions of God in their personal and corporate lives. Atheists are negative "God-Talkers." Negative "God-Talkers" engage in a theological discussion against the existence of God, His Power, His Attributes, His Character, His Son, The Holy Spirit, and Authentic Church.
- *Pastoral "God-Talkers."* These are Theologians-in-Residence, men and women who engage in talking about God and do "God-Talk" in local, regional, national, and international communities of faith. They tell the story of God through historical accounts, giving relevant messages to persons striving to positively implement "God-Talk" into their world and to continue to practice the *Insanity of Theology*. They tend to be biblical "God-Talkers" who seek to answer the question, "Is there a word from the Lord that speaks to my pain, agony, and chaos-filled world?" These

messages inspire and feed the minds, hearts, and souls of Christians as they continue to praise, worship, and put into practice the Words of the Bible, and are witnesses of God in their churches, community, and world.

- **Prophetic "God-Talkers."** These men and women are Theologians-in-Residence and Organic Theologians, on behalf of God and the people, who speak to social ills, powers, and systems that oppress the poor, the disenfranchised, and the broken. They are committed to Social Justice and remind the world that God is more concerned about how people are treated than how people praise God. They are known for speaking God's voice in the public square, seeking equality and positive action in the world.

- **Professional "God-Talkers."** These men and women engage in "God-Talk" and do "God-Talk" in the academy, seminaries, universities, and colleges. They are experts in different types of "God-Talk," including Systematic, Practical, and Liberation Theology, etc.

At the table in chair number 3, sitting to the left of me, was Dr. Howard Thurman in the person of his book *The Creative Encounter*, speaking of the importance of the "Inner Witness" and the "Inner Spark" and detailing what it means to be a believer of God. The Inner Witness, as he explained, must be fanned by the winds of God whereby the mind, heart, and soul flow like Mozart's Fifth Symphony. The Inner Spark, as he declares, must be brought to life by the actions of God and His Acts toward humankind. This concept is gleaned from the reading and causes inspiration to fill the heart. A true encounter with God causes life to change for the better, and it begins with God moving on the inside —creating the Inner Vestments and positive force on the mind, heart, and soul. This encounter results in the eruption of the "Inner Witness" and the "Inner Spark" that leads God-Talkers to a more profound inner experience, producing revelation that continues to feed the inner being to the extent of changing the person's old covering or spiritual clothing into one dressed with new Inner

Vestments, that is, attire created by the heavenly tailor who weaves anointed threads together, producing a garment that is on display in chair number 4.

In chair number 4, to the left of Dr. Howard Thurman's book, were the God-Talkers. The perpetual pursuit and the goal of every Christian is to be part of a vital church and community. Chair number 4 was actually "The Search for Inner Vestments."

The Inner Vestment of God

God-Talkers are dressed with the Inner Vestment of God as they continually study His Word and keep it in mind.
Having a working and progressive knowledge of Him.

The Inner Vestment of Christ

God-Talkers are dressed with the Inner Vestment of Christ as they seek Christ and experience Him all the more as they follow Him by faith.
Having a working and progressive belief in Christ.

The Inner Vestment of the Holy Spirit

God-Talkers are dressed with the Inner Vestment of the Holy Spirit as they seek the help of the Holy Spirit and are empowered by Him.
Having a working and progressive empowerment by the Spirit.

The Inner Vestment of the Authentic Church

God-Talkers are dressed with the Inner Vestment of the Authentic Church as they seek Her and embrace discipleship (in reach) and discipleship making (outreach).
Having a working and progressive encounter within the moving, growing, and life-changing Church.

Let's connect the dots, beginning with the Roman Catholics having made "Vestments" a central part of their worship. This conversation, inclusive of the reference to "Inner Vestments," is necessary for every God-Talker. What are Inner Vestments? They are the clothes one wears, not on their body, but on their minds, hearts, and souls. Just as one sports outer vestments/clothing on their natural bodies and changes mostly every day, Inner Vestments are images of clothing worn on their spiritual bodies. However, once applied to the spiritual body they never require changing into anything else—they are always worn. Humankind looks on outer vestments while God looks at inner vestments.

Listen to what God shared with the Prophet Samuel when he commissioned Samuel to seek out and to anoint the one who would become God's Chosen King of Israel:

> But God told Samuel, "Looks aren't everything. Don't be impressed
> with his looks and stature. I've already evaluated or elevated him."
> God judges persons differently than humans do. Men and women look
> at the face; God looks into the heart. (1 Samuel 16:7)

God is not looking to see what the God-Talkers are wearing on the outside but how they are dressed on the inside. The Inner Vestments, as highlighted in this work, are:

- *Putting God on as an Inner Vestment—Wear His knowledge*
- *Putting Christ on as an Inner Vestment—Wear His belief*
- *Putting the Holy Spirit on as an Inner Vestment—Wear His empowerment*
- *Putting the Authentic Church on as an Inner Vestment—Wear Her encounter*

One is able to see His greatness in the God-Talker's hearts when walking through the Gospel of John as he discloses, discusses, and declares knowing God, believing in Christ, being empowered by the Holy Spirit, and from encountering the Authentic Church. God will see His greatness in the God-Talker's hearts. Wearing the Inner Vestments of God, Christ, The Holy Spirit, and The Authentic Church can compel us to take on the attributes and habits of our God in our minds, hearts, and souls.

Across the landscape of this world, spiritual and worldly vestments are everywhere. If you look closely you can see them in church circles and worldly venues. "Vestments, what are they?" is the recurring question my brother Greg asked. "Please tell me more concerning Inner Vestments," he inquired. My response, as one of the God-Talkers sharing with another, is that the outer robe you wear for preaching and teaching is a vestment. Vestments in church circles are liturgical garments and articles associated primarily with the Christian faith. They're outer garments worn by clergy such as robes or cassocks while attending worship services or religious events. On the world-stage, Lil Wayne, 2 Chainz, and Rick Ross, who are Hip Hop Rap artists, have and wear vestments related to their professions. "Fear God" is tattooed on Lil Wayne's eyelids, "Two Crosses" are on 2 Chainz's gold chains, and "Ten Jesus Pieces" are around Rick Ross's neck. The outer vestment displayed on Lil Wayne's eyelids speaks to the subject of one dying to fear God. But, in reality people ought to fear God while their eyes are open, respect Him wherever one goes, and have holy reverence for God as they walk through this life. The outer vestment displayed by 2 Chainz and the crosses on each chain speak to the Crucified Savior Jesus Christ, who put our hands in God's hand, reaching out to humankind at His death and reconciling us to God. The outer vestment displayed by Rick Ross and the ten expensive heads of Christ speak to a God who forgives. However, this forgiveness starts on the inside and works its way to the outside. Vestments in worldly circles are simply religious articles and religious symbols tattooed on their bodies; the crosses and figures worn around their necks are to give an outside appearance or the impression of identification with those symbols. Church buildings can also be considered vestments, from the grand and often-palatial edifices of mega-churches arrayed in their pristine architecture to the small storefront praise parlors in old buildings, or the modestly constructed traditional cornerstone church. However, regardless of size, location, or construction, their true essence demonstrated as faithfulness and kindness are worn as the outer vestments.

I conclude this theological exploration of meanings toward the most important concept, that is, an understanding that our concerns should not be so much with outer vestments worn to impress others at a glance; they should focus on the inner vestments that radiate from within as evidence of our close relationship with the Trinity and the Authentic Church. The bridge must be crossed from outer vestments to inner vestments. If outer vestments speak to thoughts concerning God, words about God, and knowledge gained from God, should not these thoughts of theology move from the outside to the inside to change the person's mind, heart, and soul?

My late mother, God rest her soul, May Margret, was correct when she declared, "What is in you will come out of you." Can robes or cassocks, words, crosses and religious figures, and buildings heal the ills of the mind, heart, and soul? We have never heard of a robe coming out of a closet and wiping away one's tears after a life-changing event. Nor is there any notable record of a tattoo coming off the eyelids of an individual and ministering to someone after the loss of a loved one. There are no accounts of expensive jewelry making a lonely person feel secure. Nor has the God-Talker ever heard of a building moving its location to a hospital room and healing persons from a tragic vehicle accident. On the other hand, the God-Talker has heard of Inner Vestments that have evidenced themselves in powerful manifestations of kindness, love, and assurance in such circumstances. They have sustained, secured, and satisfied the inner question, "Does *Insanity of Theology* have merit in this life?" Having Inner Vestments will give birth at home, work, and service in seasons of barrenness. Wearing the Inner Vestments of God, Jesus, The Holy Spirit, and The Authentic Church are assurances that whatever life throws at the God-Talker, victory will be the result. Better still, post-traumatic growth is guaranteed if one keeps holding on to the Holy Bible: keep on praying, keep on fasting, keep on praising, keep on worshipping God, and keep on looking up to Heaven; all things will work out for one's good when God's Inner Vestments are worn.

In the last chair, chair number 5 directly in front of me, was "The Interrogator," who defiantly dismisses the claims of the other three chair participants as well as the God-Talker who sits in the first chair at the table. At stake in this wrestling match is the outcome of humanity's struggle with life's problems and with the appropriate solutions. The winner takes all, believing and having confidence in the fact that God is the same God today as He was from the beginning of time; who over and over again and again has been turning situations around for the betterment of His people. "The Interrogator" has placed everyone at the table on trial, including the God-Talker. And, what was our crime? We stand accused of Insanity! We were judged as being *insane* for thinking, believing, and standing upon the Holy Bible, for declaring Inner Vestments as the central theme and the proper attire worn by faithful Christians who over and over again affirm the reputation of God for outcomes of life's problems and hurtful circumstances.

I left Dr. Grant's class in awe of what was to come that spring semester of 1987 and my life in ministry. Theology became for me a God-Talker's paramount pursuit. If this was to come to pass, theology had to move from the halls of academia to be practiced in the Church and in the community of God-Talkers and potential proselytizers everywhere. Theology was not just for the academy and could not be stuck there just for heated discussions and lofty debates. The *Insanity of Theology* is ever-moving, always being refined, and actively being implemented in the life of God-Talkers.

The most complex and the most commonplace of definitions often explain theology. The simplest explanation contends that humanitarians are theologians (trained experts) to some degree. Consider these complex definitions: theology is science that treats the facts and phenomena of religion and relationships between God and man. Alternatively, theology is the philosophical discipline dealing with the question of God in relationship with other philosophic questions. Additionally, consider theology that is the historical analysis of the doctrine and beliefs of religion. It is often said that theology is a set of beliefs concerning God, the study of God, or the thoughts of God. Depending on what one has learned concerning God through study, what one has experienced concerning God through witnessing, and what one has spoken concerning God through testifying determines the theological base from which one operates in addressing a position on theology. What one really believes and trusts that God is or is not capable of accomplishing inside His house and outside of His

House, too, is theology. But *Insanity of Theology* does not just stop in a person's mind. It works its way to the heart, into the soul, and is acted out in a person's everyday life.

So let us refine our approach further by asking, what is Theology for God-Talkers? Simply put, it is "God-Talk" (according to my great friend The Rev. Clanton C.W. Dawson, Jr., Ph.D.); God-Talk is beliefs about God, the study of God and the expression of our feeling toward God. To learn about God's nature, character, and attributes is a lifelong pursuit. Since my journey began, there have been three burning questions in my heart, mind, and soul that I believe every born-again Christian must raise and answer. These questions cause us to be different from the world and its view of our unending search and grappling with our belief and faith in God. Theology cannot just be for trained theologians who dispel truths concerning God at ITC, Princeton, Fuller, or United Theological Seminary to students who are preparing for their "Call" to serve The Most High. No, no! Theology has to spill out into the surrounding place and inspire others in the hallowed halls of the Church, apartment halls, and house halls and down streets and around corners. These places and all others in between are where these three burning questions must be raised during the quest to live and not just exist in a devalued world:

1) What does theology really say?
2) What does theology really mean?
3) What does God want displayed in our theological lives?

Take into consideration Practical Theology, Liberation Theology, and Systematic Theology.

What does Practical Theology really say?
Practical Theology says it is theology that is applied in everyday life.

What does Practical Theology really mean?
When it comes to believing and having faith in God? Allow me to insert this post from my friend Charlotte's Facebook page, which makes it come alive: "Happiness keeps you sweet. Trials keep you strong. Sorrows keep you human. Failures keep you humble. And God keeps you going!"

No matter what comes and what goes God keeps the Christian going.
Through the tears, pains of life, disappointments
and setbacks and losses Heaven fuels us on!

What does Liberation Theology really say?
Liberation theology says God equips us to make the difference when
unjust behavior is present in economic, political, or social conditions.

What does Liberation Theology really mean?
Liberation theology means to believe and have faith in God.
There is the expectation that God stands on the side of the poor and
oppressed who spoke to Moses to tell Pharaoh to let His people go.
It speaks to the powers and principalities of today.

What does Systematic Theology really say?
Systematic Theology touts understanding and teaching
about God in an organized way.

What does Systematic Theology really mean?
Systematic Theology is to believe in a system of thought and have faith
in God, Jesus as the Son, The Holy Spirit as our sustainer, and that the
universe of power of salvation can come to everyone in it!

Practical, Liberation and Systematic Theologies as they relate to Dr. Grant's third burning question.

What does God want displayed in our theological lives?
I would submit that we should be noticeable practitioners of the
Insanity of Theology. *Insanity of Theology* promotes an ongoing
belief and faith in God to turn situations around for the betterment
of the individual, the Church, and the community,
even when the evidence points to the impossible.

Look again in chair number 1 where I sat with my definition of *Insanity of Theology,* and to my delight I do not sit alone. My definition gives much strength to hold off the demise, destruction, and digression "The Interrogator" desires to bring to the table. I'm absolutely insane enough to continue having confidence in Him to navigate all positive God-Talkers through the twists and turns of this life. This God-Talker has the kind of crazy faith to be assured He will turn our lives around for the better. We are *slightly off center* enough in the world's eyes to believe and have an unwavering faith in God who is steadfast and leads us to the spiritual exercises of doing the same thing over and over again, while each time God is making some different awareness in us, and while we are expecting God to change bad outcomes into great outcomes. He is actually calling us to change bad behaviors into obedience to His Word and is thereby changing our outcomes for good. We continue to exercise our spiritual muscles by praying, fasting, living the Christian virtues, and holding on to the promises of God, believing and having faith that He can turn our midnights into day.

The best outcome from any situation in life will come as heaven brings victory from the jaws of defeat. The God-Talker rises in the midst of the charges of being insane, theologically impractical, philosophically unhealthy, senseless, and having abnormal mental expressions and behavior patterns that make no sense to the world. And therein lies the foolishness of it all, for the perception is from those who have "broken cisterns." Meanwhile it makes perfect sense to one like Hannah (1 Samuel 1), who went every year to the temple praying for God to open her womb and bless her with children. Call her insane—and I am certain many in her community, even her family, probably did. However, her story ends with three sons and two daughters. The *Insanity of Theology* made perfect sense to Elijah (1 Kings 18), who sent his servant back seven times looking for rain in the midst of a season of drought until suddenly a small cloud was seen. Paul was equally insane (2 Corinthians 12) and prayed three times for a thorn to be removed, and God gave him something far greater than an abstraction…it was Grace! The goodness of God makes perfect sense to God-Talkers who have "fixed cisterns," that inner religion, a spark of life. It is the same *Insanity of Theology* that was brought to life by Proverbs 13:12: "Unrelenting disappointments leave you heartsick, but a sudden good break can turn things around." That "break" is the *Insanity of Theology* that God will make the heart well as one continues to hold on to the thought that, "He did it before and He will do it again!"

We come to the last chair, chair number 5 again, where "The Interrogator" sits in judgment of *Insanity of Theology*. We have arrived at that juncture in faith where the mind, heart, and soul converge concerning an authentic belief and faith in God. The mind, heart, and soul are in conversation as the Holy Spirit imparts inspiration, illumination, and illustration on the spiritual actions of The Christ. As John, the devoted follower of the Christ, would declare, "Follow Him and believe and you too will find an empty tomb." God moved away the stone and Christ is loose in this devalued world. Theology is having thoughts concerning God, feelings toward God, and knowledge of Him. Theology is "God-Talk." "The Interrogator" declared it senseless—it's insanity:

> "Individuals, churches, and communities are fooling themselves and are out of their minds to continue to Praise, Worship, and Honor an invisible God expecting a different result to the problems of life. Further, to believe and have faith in this unseen God and an unseen world, expecting the agents of such a world to change the course of one's life filled with problems and heartaches, is foolishness."

He continues his argument that a blessed and favored existence can result from doing the same thing over and over again with God and obtaining a different result is unrealistic, a fairy tale, and a waste of time. But, let us revisit chair number 2, with the three questions from Dr. Grant's class, specifically the third question which forcefully applies the crowning blow to win the wrestling match between the *Insanity of Theology* and "The Interrogator," and brings home the victory for God-Talkers. It is the third burning question dealing with theology and the perpetual pursuit and the lifelong quest that we seek to struggle with in this narrative. We will investigate attitudes and actions concerning thoughts about God, feelings about God, and the knowledge of God. The overcoming of theological blindness is to acknowledge that what we see and wear as outward garments only adorns our physical appearance and that in reality what is needed is to pay equally as much if not more attention to properly dressing our minds, hearts, and souls. A fruitful discussion on Outer and Inner Vestments hopefully will give birth to answering this third question. What does God want displayed in our theological lives?

The Gospel of John is rich with spiritual lessons. Learning being alive to God and the things of God is a lifelong pursuit. Knowing God through life's experiences with His involvement—His interaction with you through the different paths of your life—writes your story. You begin to acknowledge His voice and His ways and that's when the real journey begins. He provides the paper and pencil. You become the scribe writing down His marvelous acts and actions toward you as you realize that His wonder is all around. There will be times when the lines on your paper will not be straight but crooked because of the uncertainties that lie ahead. Experience Him afresh in your daily walk while His dew covers positive God-Talkers' world. See Him everywhere and in everything. Know the seasons of your life by the flowers blooming and the birds singing. Know the weather by the clouds that fill the sky and the sunrays that warm your skin. Know the Hand of God who writes across the universe and signs His name in Love. He is Eternal, He is the Crafter of life, and He is Lord.

Chapter 1

The God Who Writes Straight on Crooked Lined Paper

THE INNER VESTMENT OF GOD

"The quest to implement more knowledge of God
into one's personal life"

In the beginning God…Spoke…Then….atoms and molecules started the writing of an unending love story. The writer of this unending love story makes His intention perfectly clear. The Writer tells the universe of His love for His creation and gives Heaven's best to insure the creation's overall success. He created humankind from the dirt of the earth and the breath that brought man and woman to life. One awesome move then the next, until…the world began to move on the axis and God was the hand that moved the world. God's hand demonstrated His actions in history, with the first Adam and his fall; the rise of Abraham, Isaac, and Jacob; and Israel's bondage and salvation; and the fulfillment of Israel's covenant. An important thread holds the Writer's story together, namely, what is written and worn on the inside of His creation is far more important than what was written and worn on the outside.

Upon reflecting on the 28th chapter of Exodus, clothing or outer vestments were made for priests to symbolically transform them in appearance and function from the physical world into the spiritual world. Likewise, the Ephod stones of remembrance were worn to bring Israel into the holy presence of God where reconciling and basking in the Glory of God could be found. The Breastplate filled with all the names of the 12 tribes was a memorial to God, remembering the need to probe the mind of God in ways that would give guidance to His people. Beneath the Ephod and the Breastplate was another article of clothing or outer vestment. Then, headgear called the Rosette was identified as the blossom or flower to symbolize the loyalty and devotion of the one wearing the outer object around the head to depict life.

To quote a familiar colloquialism, "Clothes make the man," and in the biblical text, clothes make the priest as described in Zechariah 3:4-5. The reference here is to the filthy clothes that are removed and replaced with clean garments, bringing newness of self in appearance as well as a renewed spirit. Is it not safe to glean that clothes also make the God-Talker? The Inner clothes or vestments are what transform one from the physical world to the spiritual world and make the wearer worthy to proceed into the holy presence of God, prepared to probe the mind of God as one who is loyal and devoted to God.

The truth of the matter is simple and clear to this God-Talker. Namely, focus on learning more and more concerning the attributes of God. The Gospel of John says God created the entire universe and nothing is too difficult for Him. He created God-Talkers and is bigger and stronger than any problem that we will face. Listen to John 1:1-3:

> The Word was first, the Word present to God, God present to the Word. The Word was God, in readiness for God from day one. Everything was created through him; nothing—not one thing!— came into being without him.

Gaining more and more concerning His name, nature, person, work, and greatness is the goal. This knowledge has to be progressive in the here and now and not later.

In the Holy Bible the derivatives of the word know—known, knew, knowing, knowledge, and knoweth—are found over 1,400 times. These words are contained in scriptures that are fixed on knowing God, learning, considering, perceiving, seeing, recognizing, admitting, finding out more, and discerning God. It compels the believer to be wise and skillful in understanding the thoughts concerning God. It's not enough to be aware of God, gain information concerning God, and maintain religious practices about God. The bridge has to be crossed to having a progressive and working knowledge of Him that translates or transforms one into having a better life in this world. God's character has to become a part of one's everyday walk in this life. In the present tense, one needs to know God is a saving God, worthy of praise, worthy of hearing; to know that God executes wrath against enemies, rescues, rewards, sees, is merciful, shows, reveals Himself, destroys evil, is powerful, strong and mighty, perfect, pure, true, shields us from enemies, is giving, is gentle, preserving, living, and delivering. God is indeed Omnipresent (everywhere at the same time), Omnipotent (all powerful), and Omniscience (all knowing). A working knowledge of God becomes evident in the endless search of learning God's characteristics and experiencing the power of the Most High. Something wonderful happens within along with growing in the knowledge of God's character and awesome power as:

- He is Sovereign (doing whatever He wants without anyone's permission);
- He is Holy (radiant in every way); and
- He is Sufficient (perfect in all things).

There comes the realization that the more one knows about God the more one really does not know about God. Still, learning more and more concerning God is the number-one priority; it is the loftiest search to which one can aspire. One's greatest exploit should be the study of God!

The Holy Bible declares two thoughts and a third thought given to us by Divine Command theorists that are most important concerning knowing God or possessing a progressive and working knowledge of Him. The first significant thought is that *God is incomprehensible, unfathomable, and unconceivable to finite beings.* This is beautifully detailed in Job 11:7:

> Do you think you can explain the mystery of God?
> Do you think you can diagram God almighty?

The depth and limit of God cannot be achieved in our earthly, finite lives. God is inconceivable, perplexing and beyond understanding as Isaiah 40:18 declares:

> So who even comes close to being like God?
> To whom or what can compare to Him?

Isaiah continues in verses 25 and 26 of Chapter 40,

> So who is like me? Who holds a candle to me? says The Holy. Look at the night skies: Who do you think made all this? Who marches this army of stars out each night, counts them off, calls each by name, so magnificent! So powerful and never overlooks a single one?

The sun steps forward to testify to the character and power of God each day it is reporting for duty and displaying His Glory. Research reveals that the sun is 93 million miles from earth and average in size to other stars in the Milky Way, yet it is the right distance to sustain life on this planet. If it were 100 million miles away, we would freeze to death, and if it were 80 million miles away we would burn up. The sun is about 300 million times the size of the earth. The heat on the sun is so intense it can be likened to a billion nuclear bombs going off every second. The star Betelgeuse, pronounced similar to the movie *Beetlejuice* also shines forth to tell of God's awesome exploits. This star is 600 light years away from the planet earth and is 1,000 times the size of the sun. It stretches all the way to the planet Jupiter. To put this into proper perspective, think about how fast light travels. It travels 186,000 miles per second and to get to this planet light would have to travel in a year 5.88 trillion miles times 600 to get here. The Ring Nebula takes its turn to tell of the fact that there is no one like Him.

This star is 2,000 light years away and if you used the most advanced telescope available, you could see right into the middle of a rich blue color and a white dot. Scientists tells us that the white dot is a dying star and emits gases that create this wonderful-looking blue color and most importantly speaks to the character and power of God. As such, even in death beauty comes from Him. The wealth and scope of God can't be matched in this world or in the heavens.

The second important thought is that *God can be known but not in totality!* John describes this for us in John 14:7:

> If you really knew me, you would know my Father as well.
> From now on you do know him, you've even seen Him.

The roadmap for learning more and more concerning God is to follow Jesus the Christ-the way, truth, and life. Get to know God as stated in 1 John 5:20:

> And we know that the Son of God came so we could recognize
> and understand the truth of God. What a gift!
> And we are living in truth itself, in God's Son, Jesus Christ.

Jesus came that we could be rejoined to God, allowing Him to rub off on us through our willingness to reach for the knowledge of Him.

The third important thought is that *God's will for humankind can be known!* Divine Command Theorists state: "One may know the will of God in one of three ways: 1) by a sacred text, 2) personal experience, or 3) by the proclamation of a community of faith."[1] The Divine Command Theorists' thoughts concerning "sacred text" tell time and time again that the Holy Bible contains the word of God and therefore expresses the will of God. They argue that "personal experience" of an individual can have a "church road experience" with God, and that experience changes the entire makeup of a person. They argue that "proclamation of a community of faith" persons are surrounded by other believers' positive actions and heavenward movements, which produce better people because of the fellowship. The will of God has two components. First, the general will of God is that all humankind be saved. The second will of God is that God-given talents and God-given gifts be used to build up the Kingdom of God.

It was stated in the book *Beyond Belief* by Elaine Pagels that the knowledge of God has to be a progressive working knowledge in the here and now. Dr. Pagels has a Ph.D. degree from Harvard and teaches at Princeton. In her book, this professional God-Talker, this scholar, trained theologian, and awesome woman of God, who has devoted an in-depth study to matters concerning God and Christianity, is faced with a real-life heartache. Her story is one that shows the revitalization of a person's passion, belief, and faith toward God. Spurred on by personal tragedy, in the introduction of the book she tells of her son Mark, who has a rare lung disease. She recounts of jogging in the month of February on a Sunday morning and while working out gets cold and goes into a church to get warm. As she goes into the church and begins to warm herself she is further drawn into the house of God. Hearing the singing, praying, and inspiring message, she begins the process of moving from learning about God (belief) to gaining hope (faith) in God. She writes,

> I was acutely aware that we met there driven by need and desire, yet sometimes I dared hope that such communion has the potential to transform us.[2]

She speaks of going back to this church for strength to deal with her son's lung disease and a hope in God to make a difference in her situation. She came out of the cold to experience the warmth of God. Before going into the church, if she had been placed in a spiritual scanning machine to probe her mind, and given a spiritual MRI to examine her heart, along with a spiritual X-ray machine to see clear into her soul, the examination would have revealed that her theology may have been in need of revitalization, reinfusion, and refreshment from on High. The diagnosis would have revealed that to simply have knowledge of God, to study God and to have conversation with God, one has to move across the bridge of relationship to where theology is realized not just in the mind and intellect, but also in the heart and soul. If theology is accomplished only in the mind, then the relationship leans toward being more of a philosophy or lover of wisdom. But, for it to be experienced in thoughts of God, the study of God and authentic conversation with God-Talk, it must also be in the heart and soul. Dr. Pagels's theology grew from being in the mind to being in the heart and soul because after she walked into the church and continued going back to feel the warmth of the fire of God, after being put into the spiritual scanner, spiritual MRI, and spiritual X-ray machines, ultimately they would each bear witness to a much stronger testimony. Her passion and revitalization of belief and faith in God is moving, reassuring, and inspiring.

Developing a stronger theology that discovers hope in God can be found for the trials of this world amid a confidence in God that moves from the mind into the heart and soul. It is commendable to have a Ph.D. from Harvard and to teach at Princeton, but it is quite another more worthy aspiration to know the Person one has learned about and is teaching others about, to authentically bear testimony concerning a God who can make a positive difference when dealing with the ebb and flow of this life. The foundation for a healthy theology is found in a realization of the fact that one is led from having knowledge of God, or knowing about God, to having a working knowledge of God by having experienced God. Our achievements and accomplishments must be attributed to experiential knowledge of God.

Dr. Pagels continues in the introduction of her book and her inspiring story by saying,

> The presence of that worship and the people gathered there—
> and in a small group that met on weekdays in the church basement
> for mutual encouragement—my defenses fall away, exposing storms of
> grief and hope. In that church I gathered new energy, and resolve,
> over and over to face whatever awaited us as constructively
> as possible for Mark, and for the rest of us.[3]

For Dr. Pagels, her son, and the rest of those who are blessed and highly favored by God, over and over again we are looking to the Hand that moves the world desiring a different outcome by His Power, Presence, and Dynamic movement working on the backdrop of our lives. God continue to be with her and all God-Talkers who experience such trying of one's fortitude.

THE GOD-TALKER'S KNOWLEDGE OF GOD
"He can pull you out of the darkest of night"

The opportunity to be and become intimate with God is a challenge to say the least. The depth of His riches, wisdom, and knowledge to this Professional, Prophetic, Pastoral, and Practical God-Talker's understanding and finite mind is outside of my mental capacity. God's judgments are unsearchable and the most intelligent person cannot find out His ways. The greatness of God is staggering to the most mature Christian. Getting to know God suggests it will take forever, for we never can learn it all in this lifetime. Yet God invites us and gives us the road map to travel behind the veil and get a glimpse of Him on the journey. He meets the God-Talkers where they are, at the point of their first episode or their conception where His Spirit enters the heart. It is His desire for His creation to know Him and have a personal relationship that will produce a foundation to know Him, trust Him, and serve Him.

On Church Road in East St. Louis, Illinois, the fourth Saturday of August 1980, after He sat this Child of God down and played the clips of his past, I saw how all along God was with me working in the background, waiting for the right opportunity to reveal His presence. It was the next day, the fourth Sunday of August 1980, that I became a born-again Christian. That day, I began to engage in Theology, "God-Talk"—beliefs about God, the Study of God, and Feelings toward God. This God-Talker has moved from being a:

Provincial God-Talker – a person who engaged in God-Talk occasionally.

To now being a:
Practical God-Talker – a person who engages in talking about God seriously and on an everyday basis.

Pastoral God-Talker – a person who is a Theologian-in-Residence, who engages in talking about God and does "God-Talk."

Prophetic God-Talker – a person who is a Theologian-in-Residence and Organic Theologian who speak to social ills, powers, and systems that oppress the poor, disenfranchised, and broken, on behalf of God and the people.

Finally moving to being a:
Professional God-Talker – a person who engages in "God-Talk" and does "God-Talk" in the academy, seminaries, universities, and colleges.

I have moved from one class to another with one goal and one goal only—that of having a progressive and working knowledge of God in the here and now. Before the 4th Sunday of August 1980 I had a heart that longed for Him and He brought my soul to life. With no religious up-bringing and raw to the church scene, God came into this believer's life, not holding against me the fact that I had been born into sin, without awareness of the Great God of Abraham, Isaac, and Jacob, and ignorant to the actions of Heaven. God didn't care about that! What He did care about was that this new convert had a heart for knowing and loving Him to the extent that I would become a "God-Talker" even when I didn't even know of Him. I knew nothing of whom this God was when we met for the first time. Thirty years later, there is the acquired knowledge that knowing this God will take a lifetime, even an eternity. Although this God-Talker has only touched the surface of the Greatness of God, the God who made the Spiral Galaxy that is 30 million light years from earth and with so many stars they are likened to the grains of sand on planet Earth, I still live with a sense of AWE as it relates to Him. The process of growing in an intimate relationship with Him can be a bit intimidating. But, God still bids you and me to come to Him, even though we cannot fully know His mind. Taking a long look at the greatness of God, I immediately had to admit it's a challenge to comprehend Him. Yet, the prayer is always the same, "Let us know thy ways, that we may know thee, Oh God."

The process of the search for intimacy comes as "God-Talkers" come face-to-face with their belief and faith. Especially in times of testing and trials, knowing God as a company-keeper makes the hardships more bearable. God cannot be reduced to a manageable equation or formula. He can and oftentimes does the unexplainable just to keep us on our proverbial p's and q's—to be careful and mindful of His behavior standard. Time after time God makes known His ability to show up strong on Christians' behalf. There have been numerous times when life's problems and situations seemed to be getting the best of this "God-Talker," even causing belief and faith to waver and causing me to sink deeper and deeper into a pit of despair. However, the mourning of the night seasons cannot be avoided. Thus, the "God-Talker's" belief and faith in God declare that even in the night He is present. It matters not that the "God-Talker" is a worshipper who has reason to praise Him, for when the evil one provokes and grief becomes a close companion day and night, my belief and faith in God still echoes that He is there. There is a reassurance at work as I have learned more and more of the "Sweetener of Heaven" that changes the attacks of bitterness upon the soul and misery of heart that engender me with confidence that is strong because He is there.

The north wind (the wind of adversity) had been blowing on my inner witness, causing beliefs and faith to be at the brink of death. I have experienced two thousand seven hundred and eight days and counting since the south wind (the wind of joy and gladness) had blown on my garden—when the brightness and colors of roses, lilies, and dandelions filled the air with the sweet aromas of springtime. Three a.m. comes, and I'm wide awake, my thoughts dance across my mind to the tune of Miles Davis playing the blues. Tick tock, tick took, tick tock fills the rest of the early morning as more and more mourning awaits the start of another day. But, no it doesn't have to be this way. And yes, the curtain of night will close and the curtain of day will open again. All that can be mustered is required for the long journey to feel the Son's rays on the surface of my belief and faith. "Keep walking—a change is coming" is what this "God-Talker" told himself. Isolated are the affirmations that have been building from day one to 11,145 and counting. The atheist who is in the second class of (Practical) "God-Talkers" in a negative way believes God does not exist and there are no miracles, no signs and wonders. The agnostic in the first class (Provincial) "God-Talkers" believes maybe He does or maybe He doesn't exist. This "God-Talker" has a history with the God that rules and super rules in the universe and has power over the mourning he faces. Tears are cried and fall frozen by the time they hit the floor and pain is constant, yet I know that my intimate relationship with the Greatness of God will bring me out and the track record of God continues to be spotless. This is God writing straight on crooked lined paper! Overcoming the atheist, agnostic, and Interrogator's attacks, this Practical, Pastoral, Prophet, and Professional "God-Talker" holds on to what has been gleaned from prior experiences with God being a present help in times of testing. The closing of the curtain of night ends as God opens the curtain of day and I rejoice for the confidence that was placed in Him. The God-Talker continues to hold true to the discipline of knowing that spiritual exercise also makes the difference in growing a relationship with God and the *Insanity of Theology* (promotes an ongoing belief and faith in God to turn situations around for the betterment of the individual, the Church, and the community, even when the evidence points to the impossible) moves the Mercy Seat of God into action. Joy comes in the morning.

The Indiana Jones and the Last Crusade Knowledge of God
"Passing the tests to get closer to God"

The quest for being alive to God and the things of God are in full pursuit. It is a quest for real happiness, inner joy, and living in the spiritual realm of the eternal and not just existing in the natural realm. Moving from being in the first class of "God-Talkers" (Provincial) to second class "God-Talkers" (Practical) in a positive way, then on to those who are called to third, fourth, and fifth classes of "God-Talkers" (Pastoral, Prophetic, and Professional) requires rigorous discipline. Learning more and more concerning the subject of God comes through prayer, meditation, and trials. Praying for understanding, insight into the mysteries of God, and being able to gain knowledge of Him and how to apply that knowledge in the world of a God-Talker in positive ways must be a consistent daily exercise. Add to that asking God for aid to brave life well in the midst of heartache and pain and to be an effective "God-Talker" in word and deed. Be intentional about meditating and giving additional thought to getting to know more and more concerning the ways of God, the thoughts of God, and the movement of God. Thinking deeply on the Holy Word of the Bible and digesting a little more and more of Him in one's mind, heart, and soul daily is the key to spiritual growth. Trials do come to make Christians strong, but that strength is accomplished through the power of His might. It's a fact that beauty does come through suffering and not from the exemption from the trials of this world. Trials and tests are a part of this life, so we must allow the knowledge of God to shed light on our circumstances, just as the Christian trusts that things will become better. But in the meantime, "God-Talkers" need not become bitter! Desiring to know God is a quest for the serious "God-Talker," keeping in mind that study concerning God requires surrendering to a life-long journey. As you center on a life filled with happiness, the Christian has to read the Holy Bible and learn from and apply the lessons contained in the scriptures. For the first class of "God-Talkers" learning is just filled with reading verses, chapters, and books, but to the serious student of God those words come alive and are true no matter how bad the world becomes. The Christian understands that the only way to achieve real happiness is to cling to His precepts and hold on to His testimonies, which bring inner joy as you breathe in its holy oxygen for a healthy mind, heart, and soul.

This is the message of the third film in the Indiana Jones movie series that came alive on the big screen. Released in 1989, it was directed by Steven Spielberg and starred Harrison Ford as Indiana Jones, who was in search of the Holy Grail, a biblical artifact said to have supernatural powers. Supposedly, a person who drank from the cup was granted eternal life and youth. The Holy Grail was believed to be the cup that Jesus Christ used during the Last Supper. It was also said to be used to catch Christ's blood at his crucifixion.

This is the storyline, but what can we make of it? It is no secret that humankind is continually searching for something tangible and intangible to answer the cosmic question, "How can I live on earth and be happy?" Mary J. Blige sings the song "I Just Want to Be Happy," Pharrell Williams sings the song "Cause I'm Happy," and it's a fact that persons who walk this earth go to great lengths to gain a state of bliss. In *Indiana Jones and the Last Crusade,* a person wanted to acquire the Holy Grail and drink from the Cup of Christ to gain eternal life and youth, but pursued it with ill motives and evil desires. Conversely, Indiana Jones and his father pursued the object to acknowledge the glory of God and possessed positive desires. The key to finding and obtaining the Holy Grail in the motion picture was to pass the tests of God. The tests in order were:

- To kneel before the breath of God; only the penitent man or woman will pass.
- To walk in the footsteps of God, to walk in God's name.
- To leap from the lion's head, to take the leap of faith.

Notice that all three tests are scripturally based and theologically true. Then notice that for "God-Talkers" these three tests are crucial characteristics to have for anyone who is seeking to drink with The Christ in peace. If a "God-Talker," no matter what class he or she may be in, is going to gain eternal life and be alive to God and the things of God, all three tests must be passed. There are three major hallmarks that separate the class of "God-Talkers." The movie suggests that whoever strives to gain Christ's Cup would be one whose human characteristics have a strong theological base. The first test is that one has to be humble to be alive to God and the things of God, for only the penitent can pass. The Holy Bible speaks of humility being a characteristic of a "God-Talker." Scriptures like 2 Chronicles 7:14, Psalm 34:2, Psalm 69:32, Matthew 18:4, and Matthew 23:12 tell of the importance of being humble persons in the sight of God. By definition, to think or judge with lowliness and hence to have lowliness of mind is what being humble means. Pride exalts while humility allows one to see them as they truly are. Sinners saved by grace have learned that proud persons will be cut down but that the humble will receive what they do not deserve—the favor of God as declared in James 4:6. Humility allows you and me to act agreeably to develop harmonious relationships, thus attaining every spiritual success and every moment of joyous fellowship with the God of Heaven. The "God-Talkers" who kneel before God and walk humbly through the Breath of God will gain real happiness, inner joy, and the ultimate goal of drinking from the Cup of Christ.

The second test is something that all "God-Talkers" should pursue heartily—learning the names of God. To walk in the Path of God ensures successful travel. Only walking in the footsteps of God brings real happiness and contentment. The theological implication of walking in any other name would be disastrous, but to walk in His name assures blessed and favored foundations. The mind of a "God-Talker" should treasure His name and knowledge. The heart of a "God-Talker" transmits the inner message of who He is to the voice of the theist and makes audible the awareness of knowing Him and His name. The soul of a "God-Talker" is able to pass life's trials and tests because of knowing Him and His name.

The last test is the leap of faith. No "God-Talker" can see his or her way apart from having faith in God—walking by faith and not by sight. Faith is confidence in the promises of God, knowing that to be alive to Him and His Kingdom principles will bring sublime happiness. I remember how I felt when my birthday was approaching. I was excited and anxious. I knew I'd get birthday cards, presents, and even a yellow cake with chocolate icing. But, some things would come as a surprise. Birthdays are occasions that combine assurance and anticipation at its best, and so does faith. Faith is the sublime confidence acquired from the past experiences that promise that God's new and fresh surprises will surely be ours. The confidence and assurance that comes from knowing God will get "God-Talkers" to the point of finding the Cup of Christ, and drinking from His Holy Grail filled with the water that will never leave one in thirst.

The Avatar Ian's Knowledge of God
"Going beyond cloaked garments of religion"

Moving beyond belief and having faith in God gives hope, energy, and a new insight into gaining a healthier theology despite the level of academic preparation or exposure one has—be it a terminal degree (the Ph.D.) or an elementary education. The key, of course, is to learn more and more concerning God, which will lead to more fruitful living that crosses the bridge to having a working knowledge of Him. When one is dressed with the Inner Vestments of God, this will be the most enjoyable perpetual pursuit one can ever have in this life.

Recently, I revisited the movie *Avatar*, a 2009 American epic science action film directed, written, co-produced, and co-edited by James Cameron, and starring

Sam Worthington. The film is set in the mid-22nd century, when humans are mining a precious mineral called unobtanium on Pandora, a lush habitable moon of a gas giant in the Alpha Centauri star system. The expansion of the mining colony threatens the continued existence of a local tribe of Na'vi, a humanoid species indigenous to Pandora. The film's title refers to a genetically engineered Na'vi body with the mind of a remotely located human that is used to interacting with the natives of Pandora. Sam Worthington's character gets so close to the Na'vi that he becomes one of them without them knowing he's a double agent. He is sent in with a mission from the head of security to learn as much as he can about the Na'vi in order to gain the edge in battle and remove them from their home that is rich in unobtanium. He gets the Intel needed for the assault, but after being trained by Zoe Saldana's character, he falls in love with her and her people. He has second thoughts and decides to fight for the Na'vi because they have become a part of his life in the three places required to change one from the inside out. In his mind, heart, and soul the Na'vi became his people and he embraces their beliefs and has faith in their God Yahweh. The Avatar body he wears is an outer garment/vestment, but as he also wears the love of the Na'vi people in his mind, heart, and soul, it changes him. The most important thought about this character was his adoption of a key saying that was central to the Na'vi's culture. It is a saying that supersedes everything they say—that is the saying "I See You." This phrase can also speak to the character of our God and how like Him we should aspire to be—to see as our God sees the inside beyond the outer covering. This belief is made up of what is seen beyond the outer Avatar vestment or covering and goes to the inner dressing of God. We are made up of the inner dressings of God.

I'm sure James Cameron, if he were a boastful man, would say from the tallest mountain in Hollywood that *Avatar* broke several box office records and made more money than *Titanic*. Yet what will be priceless to the halls of Heaven is that theism did not win any Academy Awards, but *Avatar* won nine awards, breaking all box office records and changing from the inside out to fight for being dressed with God. Yes, we are to know Him not just in claims but also to know Him in conduct, compassion, correspondence, Christianity, and conviction. Jeremiah 9:23-24 says,

> Don't let the wise brag of their wisdom. Don't let heroes brag of their exploits. Don't let the rich brag of their riches. If you brag, brag of this and this only: That you understand and know me. I'm God, and I act in loyal love. I do what's right and set things right and fair, and delight in those who do the same things. These are my trademarks.

In this text three classes of men or women are mentioned:

- First class is those who brag and boast in their ability to possess knowledge and know how to apply said knowledge (yet man's wisdom is finite).
- Second class is those who brag and boast in an effort to glory in their might (even though it is limited).
- Third class is those men and women who brag and boast in their bank accounts (yet riches are temporary).

What can men or women brag, boast, and glory in as a "God-Talker"? I submit it is the essential and eternal working knowledge of God and the blessing of Him changing one from the inside out! It is knowing that God is the basis of all blessings and favor in life, here and in the hereafter. It is the condition of trust in God. The past blessing and favor were upon Him. The present blessings and favor are predicated upon Him. The future blessings and favor depend upon Him. To see and observe God in action causes transformation of old ideals and actions of false gods that promise a fruitful life yet fail in comparison in understanding and knowing God. Consider time after time expecting a skillful God who is into details, writing a new story on jagged lined paper, telling the story of a fresh destiny of the Christian as we watch from the sidelines in AWE of Him working on the "God-Talkers'" behavior and behalf. He accomplishes this as He looks to and fro in the earth, showing Himself strong on behalf of Christians all around the globe, comforting the broken-hearted in times of trouble, and exercising His power. It was clergyman Dr. Tony Evans who wrote,

Knowing God involves more than awareness, more than information, more than religious experience. To know God is to have Him rub off on you, to enter into relationship with God so that who He is influences who you are. One of the greatest tragedies today is that you can go to church and be aware of God; you can go to church and have information about God; and if your church has a great choir, you can even go to church and "feel" God; but you can leave church with Him never having rubbed off on you.[4]

Since God exercises Himself in the earth by accomplishing, advancing, and appointing His loving-kindness, judgment, and righteousness, the "God-Talker" ought to work with Him by declaring that we too have the same qualities because He has rubbed off on us. We too ought to have loyal love like God who hangs in there with us even when we don't hang in there with Him. We too ought to be fair and treat others with fairness. The Rev. Dr. Martin Luther King, Jr. was correct when he said, "The arc of the moral universe is long, but it bends towards justice."[5]

THE 12 YEARS A SLAVE KNOWLEDGE OF GOD
"We're not exempt but not alone either"

The problem with a devalued world is that even though in the universe God will always be fair when others will not be, the influence of evil is ever present. Therefore, to be clothed with the armor of God is always the Christians' best bet. God is the only One who can:

- Bring two million of His people from the wretched hands of a pharaoh;
- Deliver three young men from the unjust sentence of being thrown into a fiery furnace for standing on divine principles;
- Watch over a servant all night long in the presence of hungry lions and continue His unblemished record by doing the unheard of—raising His Son from the clutches of Satan with all power in His hand.

God has the uncanny ability to close the curtains of night and open the curtains of day. The north wind of adversity has to go and blow no more as the south wind of joy and gladness blows on the situation that has left one in the dark and in the midst of a wilderness situation. Light that shines in dark places and human events and life experiences are welcome to the one who has to endure the contemptible, crafty, and conquering cruelness of others, as shown in the movie *12 Years a Slave*. In the pre-Civil War United States, Solomon Northup, a free black man from upstate New York, is abducted and sold into slavery. Facing cruelty at the hands of a slave-owner, as well as unexpected kindnesses, Solomon struggles not only to stay alive, but to retain his dignity. In the twelfth year of his unforgettable odyssey, Solomon's chance meeting with a Canadian abolitionist would forever alter his life. Chiwetel Ejiofor, who plays the main character Solomon Northup, also comes to a very real reality, namely, there is a major benefit in calling on the name of God in the midst of such an unbearable situation. The injustices of Jewish concentration camps, the endless wars in Africa and other nations, and African Americans' 400 years of slavery together reveal one constant truth: The braving of the storms of life comes from the inner presence of an experiential knowledge of God. Solomon exemplified this as he goes through his ordeal of being sold into slavery for 12 long years and his neverending prayer to God to deliver him from this nightmare. Forced into a life of unending servitude, he embraced God's power to turn his situation around, knowing that he'd see his family again. He never lost faith in God to bring him through, knowing God made the difference.

In the darkness, the wickedness, and the injustices of this world, a "God-Talker" has to know God from an intellectual knowledge and from an experiential knowledge of God. Knowledge of the supreme God, the strong creator, the one who stepped out on nothing and made this world with His Word and it come into existence, is critical. Daniel called Him Elohim, the strong Creator who is a person with self-awareness, intellect, and emotions and can be trusted to use His energy to hold us together until aid comes to turn our situations around. This is why the confidence in Elohim should not waiver in the face of great trials, especially when He is the Christians' only refuge and present help in times of trouble. Trouble knows where every person in this world lives, and without the warning of email, Twitter, and Facebook alerts God is the best protection from the injustices of this life. Because of the first Adam's sin, humankind will never be exempt from the rough side of the mountain in this life. Because of the second Adam's sacrifice on the Cross, Christians everywhere are infused with the force from within to endure hardship like soldiers, until God intervenes in our situations that have made the Christian a slave to the unfavorable experiences in this life. It provides the strength and superior ability to go through bad situations and smile while it's occurring, mainly because of being confident in the One who will bring fairness back to the mind, heart, and soul of a loyal follower of the Kingdom. Daniel 11:32 declares,

> Those who stay courageously loyal to their
> God will take a strong stand.

Life is not a bed of roses, skies will not always be blue, and the storms of sickness will come into the theist world. Yet the proper posture for you and me is simply to "Hold on to your faith in God" to carry one through the very rough patches of this life. When confronted with the issues of life, know that God's Grace is sufficient!

Corrie ten Boom, a Dutch Christian, along with her father and other family members, helped many Jews escape the Nazi Holocaust during World War II and was imprisoned for it. This great woman of God and her family loved, respected, and followed God, and during the Jews' night experience built a room on their home to hide them. Her family got caught and they too were sent to the camps. Most of her family died during the ordeal, yet when Corrie was free she was quoted as saying, "There is no hole that is so deep, that God is not deeper still."[6]

Horrible predicaments, vile, foul, horrible, and wicked situations must be met with partnering with God to ensure the "God-Talker" who is a Christian comes forth from darkness and suffering having held on to his or her faith in Him. All of God's "God-Talkers" must do just as Corrie ten Boom's family did and become soldiers who have to toughen up to fight from the inside out in the face of fires of persecution. The call from Heaven is to endure hardships. Crises serve to reveal the genuineness of a born-again believer's faith. We know that our partner in the catastrophic challenges of life is God! Furthermore, knowing God is to take life head-on with the confidence that Heaven will not let you fight alone. Join God in partnership when faced with ugly circumstances that will always be present in this life. As you and I undergo overwhelming suffering at times we can take on the Nike® saying, "Just do it." Why should we do it and endure? Because we are not the only ones who have to endure the ugliness of life, and as the great cloud of witnesses would testify it's all a part of being part of the Kingdom of God. The Child of God is not exempt from the trials and tribulations of this journey. He just makes sure that you and I do not have to settle for "existing" in life but "living" a more abundant life.

THE BOOK OF ELI KNOWLEDGE OF GOD
"Take the Word on your journey"

The person who thinks after giving his or her hand to a pastor and his or her heart to God that everything will be smooth sailing is in for a rude awakening. The person who believes like this is setting himself or herself up for a major downfall. God doesn't operate like that. He is not a celestial jack-in-the-box that will magically pop out by winding the handle. To be alive to God and the things of God comes from a working knowledge of Him. This offers life that's endless, a quality of existence that is privileged and an honor, divinely endowed with the ability to know God. The Practical, Pastoral, Prophetic, and Professional "God-Talkers" are supernaturally imparted with a new standard, new values, and new ideals for life that come from crossing the bridge to life that is lifelong and that begins and ends with God. After encountering God's standard of measurement there should be the Christian standards and scale of values. Learning of such thoughts gives one the progressive knowledge needed to learn more and more concerning the Only True God every day, for in this world there are false, pagan, and unreal gods. Knowing and learning more about God every day is the key to experiencing His works and deeds.

This theme truly played out in the 2010 movie *The Book of Eli*, starring Denzel Washington. This post-apocalyptic action film revolves around Eli, a nomad who is told by a voice to deliver his copy of a mysterious book to a safe location on the West Coast part of the United States. This mysterious book later is discovered to be the last known King James Bible in existence. The history of the post-war world is explained along the way, as is the importance of Eli's task. He says he was led to the book by a voice in his head, which then directed him to travel westward to a place where it would be safe. The voice assured him that he would be protected on his journey. Thus, for 30 years he has been traveling west, guided by his faith. Later Eli is revealed to be blind and begins to dictate the Bible from memory before his death. Denzel Washington's character was on an endless journey and quest to not only carry the last Bible in his post-war travels to the west coast, but to learn from it, meditate upon it, and let it take hold of his mind, heart, and soul.

The Holy Bible is more than just chapters, books, and wise words to be researched; it is to be learned and to be lived by. It is life to the "God-Talker," especially to the breathing of spiritual lungs, and signs, wonders, and miracles that come alive, from the pages of the most influential words ever written. The words come alive moving in the Christians' world, bringing the missing ingredient that makes life worth living. God's words interacting with the Christian and the experiences the "God-Talker" faces on a daily basis bring a sense of calm to the storms we all will face. To have God's words bring life on the backdrop of death, bring blessings and not cursings and real solutions to the ills of an imitator of Heaven's world, is priceless.

Eli was on a constant journey of learning, living, and acting on a book that has all the answers to the greatest subject one can study. The Only True and Living God that is fresh every moment of the day. The God who has eyes and can see, ears and can hear, arms and can reach. It was Charles Spurgeon who said,

> I believe that the proper study of God's elect is God. The proper study of a Christian is the Godhead. The highest science, the loftiest speculation, the mightiest philosophy which can ever engage the attention of a child of God is the name, the nature, the person, the work, the doing and the existence, of the great God whom he calls his Father.[7]

Every day should be a day to learn something new about a God who continues to reveal more and more of Himself to the walker of faith. Eternal life by definition points to this fact. The quality of existence and the divine, endowed ability to be alive to God and the things of God is the goal. It stresses the principle and condition to life eternal, to know God as He really is and all that flows from that. John 17:3 says, "That they know you, the one and only God."

The God that won on Mt. Carmel as the prophet Elijah called down the fire in 1 Kings 18:21 or the God who has substance from Psalm 115 cannot be defeated. Yet the key to knowing God is more than grasping the meaning of being alive to Him. The meaning should cause a reaction from the inside moving on to the outside toward living a life that is after God's way, and a life that's lived in eternity.

The 47 Ronin Knowledge of God
"Devotion to our King"

The constant fight of the children of the King is to never forget that salvation is free but that there is still a cost to pay, namely, the fight to put into practice what is learned of God. It's not enough to be on the path of knowledge of God but to walk the path of having knowledge of God. Gleaning from the field of the heavens is work in itself and to continue will take sacrifices of time, talent, treasure, opportunity, and influence. This requires fixing thoughts in mind, heart, and soul with diligence, earnestness, and sincerity to go the extra mile in service to the Kingdom of God, leaving behind traits of old. Laying aside one's own agenda and picking up the Throne's agenda is not child's play. Setting aside time to steal away with Him and His Word instead of watching the cliffhanger of *Scandal* may be the order of the day. To gain a higher spiritual IQ in the mind requires alone-time with the Master. This will insure obtaining a greater level of understanding in heart. It means taking out sin and replacing it with the fruit of the Spirit. Springing forth from the soul, which goes higher and higher obtaining new heights, will only occur as greater altitudes are climbed. Yes, it's a fact that some things in our personal lives must decrease so that the "God-Talker" can increase, not for our sakes, but for the Kingdom's sake. The aim of the child of the King is gain and loss…gains more for the Kingdom of God and more loss of the Kingdom of this world. To serve God as Master will cost every spiritual person just as serving Satan as master of this world will cost an expensive price. Paul called for placing his or her life in the Hand of the Master when he wrote Romans 12:1-2,

> Embracing what God does for you is the best thing you can do for him. Don't become so well adjusted to present-day culture that you fit into it without even thinking. Instead, fix your attention on God. You'll be changed from the inside out.

When the movie *47 Ronin* hit the big screen, I went to see this epic motion picture and Paul's words came to life: serving another by putting one's life in their hands. *47 Ronin* is a 2013 American fantasy action film depicting a fictional account of a real-life group of Samurai in the 18th century of Japan who avenge the murder of their master. Starring Keanu Reeves as the main character, Kai, an outcast and illegitimate son of a British sailor and a Japanese peasant woman, joins a group who seeks vengeance on a ruthless man who killed their master and banished the group of 47 loyal men. The Ronin Samurai embarks on a journey with challenges that would defeat most warriors. But because of their loyalty to the cause and master they were willing to give their lives for service.

Keanu Reeves's character, along with the others, depicts the extent a servant is willing to serve their master and the Ronins put their lives in the hands of the master to serve their cause. Their determination and will was not their own but to one who was being served. The cost of the journey is to be noted because it has merit in the "God-Talkers'" perpetual pursuit to serve God. Serving God is not a hallowed event on a certain day of the week, but every day of the week. Dietrich Bonhoeffer wrote in *The Cost of Discipleship* about Costly Grace versus Cheap Grace:

> Cheap grace is the deadly enemy of our Church. We are fighting today for costly grace. Cheap grace means grace sold on the market like cheapjack's' wares. The sacraments, the forgiveness of sin, and the consolations of religion are thrown away at cut prices. Grace is represented as the Church's inexhaustible treasury, from which she showers blessings with generous hands, without asking questions or fixing limits. Grace without price; grace without cost![8]

No Ronin would ever serve his master with cheap grace. The "God-Talkers," Church, and community strive for a deeper dedication to the cause of God. Costly Grace has to be the order of the day every day. Salvation is free but it costs the Christian every day. It costs sacrifice and the renovation in the heart, mind and soul. It takes commitment and reverence that Christians willingly pay as their reasonable service to God. For God the "God-Talkers" live, and for God the Christian dies.

Costly Grace is what the "God-Talkers" pay for salvation and servitude to our God. Vital to the Church and community you and I move across the bridge from a cheap-lived relationship with God to the other side of the bridge where living costs so much more. Costly Grace means so much more than to use God's grace as a license plate to do one's own bidding, but it is used to do the bidding of the Master. Bonhoeffer continues by saying,

> Costly grace is the gospel which must be sought again and again and again, the gift which must be asked for, the door at which a man must knock. Such grace is costly because it calls us to follow, and it is grace because it calls us to follow Jesus Christ. It is costly because it costs a man his life, and it is grace because it gives a man the only true life. It is costly because it condemns sin and grace because it justifies the sinner. Above all, it is costly because it cost God the life of his Son: "Ye were bought at a price," and what has cost God much cannot be cheap for us. Above all, it is grace because God did not reckon his Son too dear a price to pay for our life, but delivered him up for us. Costly grace is the Incarnation of God.[9]

To fight for the cause of the Kingdom will cost the children of the King dearly and shortcuts are not an option. From the inside out Costly Grace is carried out as an offering to God from the Christian who serves the Master out of Holy Reverence.

God-Talker's Golden Rule
"Living life like it's golden"

No one can make it in this world alone! Since theology is not exclusive to the halls of theological education or academia, it is a true fact that anyone can be a "God-Talker." A theologian is a Pastoral, Prophetic, and Professional "God-Talker" who is an expert in theology. Persons in the Professional, Prophetic, Pastoral, and Practical "God-Talkers" (in a positive manner) are persons who move from being a novice or a beginner in belief and faith in God to moving to being more advanced in word and deed. Or as Peter put it best,

> You've had a taste of God. Now, like infants at the breast, drink deep of God's pure kindness. Then you'll grow up mature and whole in God. (1 Peter 2:2)

The little old lady in tennis shoes with an 8th grade education, who has moved from drinking milk to eating the meat of the word; the cocaine-addict CEO in a Brooks Brothers tailored suit, who moved from being high on drugs to being high on knowing God; and the guy hustling on the corner learning it's better to push God than dope—all can have thoughts concerning God. There are "God-Talkers" at the barber and beauty shops on any city street corner. "God-Talkers" who frequent Starbucks speak about God over coffee and caramel apple spice cake with whipped cream, and in YMCA steam rooms God is spoken about in awesome testimonies of triumph. To believe and have faith in God is somewhat unusual, but what is truly unusual is having a working knowledge of God that crosses the theological bridge and overcomes theological blindness, thus transcending this mundane world and moving beyond it to the world of endless possibilities with God. I have always wanted to ask the late, great Maya Angelou, who wrote the poem "Alone," if God crossed her mind, and did her soul scream, "You need God in this life"?

Alone

"Lying, thinking / Last night / How to find my soul a home
Where water is not thirsty / And bread loaf is not stone
I came up with one thing / And I don't believe I'm wrong
That nobody / But nobody / Can make it out here alone.
Alone, all alone / Nobody, but nobody / Can make it out here alone.

There are some millionaires / With money they can't use
Their wives run round like banshees / Their children sing the blues
They've got expensive doctors / To cure their hearts of stone.
But nobody / No, nobody / Can make it out here alone.
Alone, all alone / Nobody, but nobody / Can make it out here alone.

Now if you listen closely / I'll tell you what I know
Storm clouds are gathering / The wind is gonna blow
The race of man is suffering / And I can hear the moan,
'Cause nobody, / But nobody / Can make it out here alone.

Alone, all alone / Nobody, but nobody / Can make it out here alone.[10]

The theologian in me the "God-Talker" screams out with a loud voice: "Getting a progressive and working knowledge of God is needed to find one's mind, heart, and soul a home in God." To believe and have faith in God is the only way to assure that as the storm clouds blow and the suffering of humankind continues, "God-Talkers" have a partner who is present and who can brave life with us, and where success takes a back seat to being faithful to God. My heart breaks as people try in vain to handle the challenges of this life by themselves. Preachers who have knowledge of God but not a progressive and working knowledge of God are found dead because of self-inflicted gunshot wounds or in a hotel room overdosing on illegal substances. Pew members who have knowledge of God but not a progressive and working knowledge of God are left in the nighttime experiences trying to find solutions to their hurt and pain, becoming addicted to the wine of this world, staggering like a drunken believer. Where was and is their progressive and working knowledge of God? Their Inner Vestment of God was and is absent, but outer vestments of cars, money, perverted sex, and clothes were present. The call of heaven is to get God on the inside to be the anchor we all need. Stop putting so much faith in things and put one's faith in a healthy theology, which is passionate and invigorating and crosses the bridge to a better future with God as its foundation, fortune, and future.

In the Gospel of John, He is in a class all by Himself. His uniqueness spells out words that all can understand. The Anointed One is loose in the World to clearly and accurately give us the GPS directions to Heaven. He provides turn-by-turn directions to assist all lost travelers with the right directions to see how to navigate through a world with so many wrong turns. Lost? Pull over and read the map. The Holy Bible is your map. Run into a roadblock? A way to go around will be provided. Look for His Signs. Faced with construction delays, rest in the assurance that trouble ahead will be taken care of. Detour sign up ahead? He will give the best alternative route available. Dead-end Street in your view? Don't worry—there's no such thing with Him. Trust His judgment. Lean on His expertise. Rely on His ability to get you safely to Heaven's destination. Christ is the God-Man and the Revealer-Redeemer who moves down your street. He knows the way Home.

Chapter 2

The Savior Who Travels Down Dead-End Streets

THE INNER VESTMENT OF CHRIST
"The journey to be more like Him in a devalued world"

The day God pitched His tent in this world and spoke the words, "Let there be...," galaxies whirled into place as stars and planets danced around the sun. Waters and lands filled open spaces as creatures ran and swam, growing and multiplying. He kissed the dirt and man and woman came to life, thinking, breathing, and pulsing with natural and divine activity. In the first dispensation period, the God who pitched His tent in this world, the Eternal One full of infinite power and unlimited resources, commanded that movements fall into silence. The interlinear period where He says nothing for four hundred years speaks. Through the womb of a virgin, in the heart of a carpenter and in a smelly stable filled with farm animals, God's Number One unveils Himself in marvelous acts toward His creation. To Christians all around the globe, in their mind, hearts, and souls, the Maker of all existences unveils His greatest secrets in the second dispensation period. In this Person of love personified and adoration incarnate, affection multiplies as the heavens marvel at His Handy Acts. The life-giving Son of God steps onto the scene from behind the covering of infinity, revealing grace and truth. It is from this entrance that the refiner of hearts moves down the king's highway meeting people from all walks of life, preaching and teaching to crowds who are changed from the inside out. He is a molder of followers who are in constant battle with evil but who come to worship Him in spirit and truth. As truth steps from behind the veil and through His eyes, the light of God shines bright, the voice of God is heard in different notes of love, and the One out front cries,

> "My flesh becomes the tent and my glory is the inner tent through which grace and truth can be seen all around the globe."

It is not enough to simply acknowledge grace and truth. There must be a bridge of understanding that must be crossed through experiencing His grace and His truth that makes it the number-one priority. This means that positive God-Talkers are constantly believing, having faith and trusting Christ and continually believing and relying on His grace and truth. Believing must be active and trust is continuous in the process of living the life of born-again Christians. The "God-Talker" acts on a belief that arises from the surety and acceptance of Christ's life, death, and resurrection, causing a change from the inside out. This belief comes alive as a direct result of the power and love that bursts from His Presence. It is this progressive "believing" that has to be working within the mind, heart, and soul of the Christian, even though misunderstood and unappreciated in a devalued world.

The words believe, believers, belief, and believing occur roughly 500 times in the Holy Bible. These words are centered on actively trusting and exercising faith in Christ. Worthy of consideration is the meaning for the words belief and faith. The meaning is different in the English dictionary and in the Greek. In the Greek text the words focus on the *action* of believing. The *actions* of believing are the stepping-stones that lead the "God-Talker" across the bridge to *continual* believing and having faith in Christ's ability, thus giving birth to the trust that does not waver. Trusting in Him provides you and me with the ability to gain aid either in obtaining what is needed or desired or in doing something that no one else can do by giving oneself up to His will. One's belief is preserved, strengthened, increased, and raised to levels it ought to reach to secure an optimal result.

As conviction of what one believes encourages inner actions to be taken, change also begins to take place outwardly in expressions or conversations and actions or conduct. The law of the soul is experienced from the inside out living in harmony with the Holy Bible, believing in Christ's purpose for coming into this world. It is belief that is vigorously moving, aggressively acting from the inside out, dynamically and progressively working until Heaven's purpose is reached, as the Apostle John declared in John 20:30-31:

> Jesus provided far more God-revealing signs than are written down in this book. These are written down so you will believe that Jesus is the Messiah, the Son of God, and in the act of believing, have a real and eternal life in the way he personally revealed it.

Believe, believers, believing, and belief in Christ must come in two important facts. The first fact is gleaned through His Works or Signs or Miracles or Wonders that expose the grace of Heaven's earthly mission and fuels the Christian's belief. As a diamond refracts or deflects different bands or shades, so does my inner refraction, the Spirit at work in me, exemplifying different shades of God's Glory, which are unequaled throughout the universe. The perfection and completeness of God show His true shades, and no one, no prize-winning novelist or award-winning motion picture can ever surpass His attributes regardless of how meticulous and artistically well-composed their works may be! For the Christian, His Works/Signs/Miracles/Wonders have given genuine meaning to the wonders of:

- Turning water into wine (John 2:1-12).
- Healing the nobleman's daughter (John 4:46-54).
- Healing a lame man at the pool of Bethesda (John 5:1-17).

- Feeding the 5,000 (John 6:1-14).
- Walking on the water and stilling the storm (John 6:15-21).
- Healing the man blind from birth (John 9:1-41).
- Raising Lazarus from the dead (John 11:17-45).

The Christian has just cause to travel with The Savior, namely, to consider the reasons God pitched His tent in the minds, hearts, and souls of His creation. Here is an excellent place to pause and pull back the curtain of Heaven and witness from the inside out the actions of Christ from a personal perspective. As Christ's activities penetrate the mind, heart, and soul of the born-again Christian, there are opportunities to experience the joy and source of life, the provider of healing across distances despite road blocks, the master of time and space constructively dealing with sin and suffering, the satisfier of physical and spiritual hunger, the calmer of storms and thunder, the bringer of light into dark places and possessor of the power over cursing by making them blessings. His works speak to His never-ending supremacy over the first Adam and all that followed The Fall.

The second fact is learned through His Words that show the truth of Heaven's earthly mission and propels the fan and follower of Christ. The "I Am" Chronicles of the Christ offer a portrait of unique colors from which the Christian can step back and marvel at how the statements inspire recipients of truth to become a part of divine activity in motion. Such inspiration makes it theologically clear that:

- He is the bread of life (John 6:35).
- He is the light of the world (John 8:12; 9:5).
- He is the door (John 10:7).
- He is the good shepherd (John 10:11, 14).
- He is the resurrection and the life (John 11:25).
- He is the way, the truth, and the life (John 14:6).
- He is the vine (John 15:1).

These all speak volumes of benefits to the believing Christian. Thus, it is the heartfelt reconciliation that theologically "God-Talkers" are the imitators of Christ's nourishment, vision, care, resource, victory, and progress. All of these attributes of belonging are the colors on the tapestry of life that paint a beautifully sublime picture to be enjoyed by positive God-Talkers—having life through the abundant life-giving words of Christ.

The revelation of God is revealed as the tabernacle of God is with the believer. Not in the wilderness, not in the city, not in a country, but in the center of the Christian life. Through the veil comes the voice of Heaven—Christ being the Word made flesh, the "Logos." The sayings of God are now wrapped in human flesh speaking in words that pierce the very essence of one's being. The Logos is active in creation, revelation, and redemption. These are teachings that answer the cosmic question, "Is life worth living?" As the Logos, Jesus Christ is God in self-revelation (Light) and redemption (Life). He is God to the extent that He can be present to man, knowable to man, and the One who can make the difference for man by making life worth living. He can be described as being:

- The Light that shines through darkness and gives illumination;
- The Life that gives new birth and power to become God's own;
- The Word that became flesh as the truth of God;
- The Son that came full of grace to restore and full of truth to reveal.

These four metaphors—Light, Life, Word, and Son—describe what is behind the veil. As Light He is illuminator, revealer, and expresser—He is the Word. As Life He is imparter, spark, personal Savior—He is Life.

In a devalued world, faith beliefs and belief systems are in the rear-view mirror of the imitator of Christ, but in the life of faith with a front view are affirmations that bring life. The atheist's beliefs dissent, the agnostic's beliefs are neutral, and the Christians' beliefs assent and affirm a strong belief and faith system that is not of this world. The Christian by definition is a resident alien—a foreigner who is a permanent resident of the country in which he or she resides but does not have citizenship. We are in this world but not of this world. From the worldly perspective, the theist has strange beliefs accompanied by strange actions—believing and having faith in Christ's works and words. We are not of this devalued world but we are of a higher calling that is not of this world.

Story has it that there was a blackout in New York and in the mist of darkness there was one light that was still burning bright. The Statue of Liberty—that colossal neoclassical sculpture on Liberty Island in the middle of New York Harbor, in Manhattan's New York City—was still shining bright. Someone asked how it is that she still can have electricity/power when all the rest of New York is having a blackout. The answer was that Lady Liberty receives her electricity/power from another source—the state of Pennsylvania! We are resident aliens residing in this world that is in the dark yet we receive our light, our power source from the heavens. In the book *Resident Aliens,* Stanley Hauerwas and William H. Willimon write:

> We believe that things have changed for the Church
> residing in America and faithfulness to Christ demands that we either
> change or else go the way of all compromised forms of the
> Christian faith. The Church is a colony, an island of one culture
> in the middle of another one. In baptism, our citizenship is transferred
> from one dimension to another and we become, of whatever
> culture we find ourselves, resident aliens.[1]

Christians' beliefs are to transcend in the midst of a culture that does not believe the signs and wonders of a Christ who performs miracles not to impress anyone but rather to meet the needs of the Christian. Despite not being exempt from the ebb and flow of life, we can at least be encouraged by the fact that wearing Christ we will never have to face the challenges of being a resident alien alone. In this dark world, you and I can shine bright because our source of strength comes from the power in the heavens. Leaning on the strong evidence which proves the grace and truth of Christ surpasses the acid test of the rational mind, sincerest of heart, and purest of souls is the truth that God exists and is actively involved in the human and spiritual affairs of the Child of God all around the globe. The born-again Child of the King is in the world, but from another world holding strong to beliefs in His works and His words.

THE GOD-TALKER'S REMIX VERSION OF BELIEF IN CHRIST

"Out of the picture frame and into the world"

His works and words transcend the pages of the Holy Bible. They come alive and move as the wind and air, not seen by the natural eye but by the spiritual eye that sees faithfulness, spiritual success, and spiritual growth—hallmarks in the world of all who hold true to the faith. A progressive and working belief is always in need of further motivation. Both the human and spiritual affairs of the "God-Talker" have to be on Heaven's agenda and complemented by works and words required to produce a strong incentive to keep winning and be on the move toward Heaven.

I was present the day two of the world's most articulate spokesmen took the stage to debate the topic "The Color of the Christ." The topic was the subtitle to what surfaced as the greatest title lesson ever learned. Specifically, the "God-Talker's" life requires not the color of Christ painted in a picture frame but a colored Christ whose multitude of colors elicit strokes of power and life-changing presence that come alive outside of a picture frame in the hearts, souls, minds, and world of the resident aliens.

Molefi Kete Asante (born Arthur Lee Smith, Jr.) is an African American scholar and historian who has authored of over 70 books and 400 articles. He is a professor of African American Studies at Temple University and President of the Molefi Kete Asante Institute for Afrocentric Studies. There was an occasion when Dr. Asante was debating Dr. Cornel West, the renowned African American philosopher, academic, activist, actor, and author. Dr. West has spoken all over the world, lecturing on subjects like Nihilism (the lovelessness, meaninglessness, and hopelessness that is prevailing in streets across the globe), and was the first African American to graduate from Princeton with a Ph.D. in philosophy. The debate went on for an hour. Back and forth they went at each other on the subject "The Color of the Christ." I witnessed Dr. Asante scoring the most points as Dr. West tried to get a word or two in edgewise. Dr. Asante was winning the debate until the moment when Dr. West mentioned his grandmother's experience with the white portrait of Jesus that was in the church vestibule. Dr. West, according to those who were in attendance, told of the turning point in the debate as he said, and I'm paraphrasing,

> My grandmother, who experienced racism, plantation's horrors, and rape—when she looked at that white, long-haired and blue-eyed Jesus, saw compassion and she did not care that he was white or black. She cared that He cared for her in all of her pain.[2]

His color is relevant but not the most important thought for our discussion. What is relevant is that He can come alive to the "God-Talker" and bring calm to things that are beyond a grandmother's control. I took from the debate that Christ's skin color means nothing compared to the knowledge of receiving Christ's compassion as it comes out of the picture frame and into the world of this believer. Understanding The Compassion of Christ brings with it so much more than color, because along with the compassion of Christ comes His works, words, reputation, legions of angels, the ear of God, the great crowd of witnesses, and God Himself. The remix occurs as His compassion and all of the other characteristics of God come off the canvas of the painting and into the heart, mind, and soul of the Christian while traveling through roadblocks, detours, and dead-end streets. An animated, thriving, flourishing, and aware Christ releases His attributes into the world of a lost traveler, creating endless possibilities because nothing is impossible for Him. Moving behind the scenes, working out details for the good of His friends, and repairing the pot-holed streets of life, filling them with what's needed to make them smooth again—that is the incredible bonus of relationship with the Christ who moves beyond the picture frames hanging on the wall. I learned to never laugh at His presence or His endless and multitudinous ways of bringing impossibility into the world as He did with Sarah; never murmur, as did Moses and the children of Israel, who came across on dry land, got to Marah, and then were not able to drink the water because of its bitter taste; never doubt, as did the woman who built a house on the side of her home for the prophet of God, and He blessed her womb with a child; and never question the instructions given from the Throne, assured that the situation will change as it did with the "weeping" Prophet Jeremiah.

Consequently, as Christ steps out of the canvas onto the natural and spiritual walls of our lives, His word and His works are enlivened to change the world of the Christian for the better.

It was this Christ who Dr. West's grandmother referred to. It was a buzzing and booming Christ who is not confined but moves beyond the picture frames into the very existence of His people and thus becomes alive and operative in the life of little old ladies. Grandmother West's progressive and working belief in the Christ called Him out of the symbolism of the picture frame into active duty of human and spiritual affairs of the believer.

You and I must expect to be caught between the forces of good and evil and to face the depths of the deep Red Sea in route to the Promised Land with seemingly no way to escape or win the battle. It is at that time when His works and words leap from the sacred reserve of faith and into the secular circumstance to hold back the waters of night-long despair and lead trapped God-Talkers to walk across on dry land. It is through the manifestation of these day-to-day, whether commonplace or grandiose, miracles, signs, and wonders all around those true believers in the Moses of Moses (The Christ) that we continue to benefit from the spiritual reservoir of God's blessings and are reinforced for further challenges in the world, with increasing strength and fortitude for progressing against the "Prince of the Air." It is at this juncture that many "God-Talkers" would turn the discussion toward the real issue of life, which is how to find solace in faith without having to encounter or succumb to defeat. How does the born-again Christian garner such a strong hold on faith that it repels any unbelief or fear of things that are out of our human control? By having the right perspective!

This enemy will attack the very core of a belief system in the Christ. It is our responsibility to let His work and words come alive in this day and time. Off the colored canvases allow *Footprints in the Sand* by Mary Stevenson, a positive God-Talker, to come alive:

> One night I dreamed I was walking along the beach with the Lord.
> Many scenes from my life flashed across the sky.
> In each scene I noticed footprints in the sand.
> Sometimes there were two sets of footprints,
> other times there were one set of footprints.
>
> This bothered me because I noticed
> that during the low periods of my life,
> when I was suffering from
> anguish, sorrow or defeat,
> I could see only one set of footprints.
>
> So I said to the Lord,
> "You promised me Lord,
> that if I followed you,
> you would walk with me always.
> But I have noticed that during
> the most trying periods of my life
> there have only been one
> set of footprints in the sand.
> Why, when I needed you most,
> you have not been there for me?"
>
> The Lord replied,
> "The times when you have
> seen only one set of footprints,
> is when I carried you."[3]

Her words point to the very fact that there are times when humans can have the wrong perspective. To think that Heaven sits back and allows its residents to go the path of life in an ever-changing and unpredictable world unaccompanied is impractical, senseless, and ridiculous. Although the silence and appearance of aloneness can be unbearable, the reality is that even when Heaven is silent it does not mean that Heaven is absent. The wrong perspective is to think the theist carries the load of burdens alone and is thereby laboring under an illusion of arrogance that human strength is prevailing. There are some things in this life that are on the other side of believers' finite God-given talents and gifts—the infinite power from the heavens. Our sanctified minds beckon us to resist the temptation of being strong enough on our own to handle the trials and tribulations of this world. The lyrics to the song ring true, "No man is an island, no man stands alone," and I might add or can make it on their own. The temporary benefits of this life will ultimately not suffice: money will fail us, health will deteriorate us, friends will come and go, but we can count on the Savior to always be there—walking with Him with the promise never to leave or forsake Him. It is a mistake to think that you and I carry ourselves through difficulties when in essence it is throne-dispatched angels to the rescue. The divine perspective is found in remixing His works and words to this present age and coming to the conclusion that leaving Him in the sacred pages of the scripture is a grave mistake. The fresh, alive, vibrant, and lively Christ traffics the world looking to carry theists who cannot carry themselves. He can and will carry us and it will not happen until we invite Him off the pages of Holy Scriptures and into this fragmented and undervalued world.

Vital to the Christian, community, and Church is a Christ who not only comes out of the frame but also allows His colors to flow out into the streets. His colors of love, forgiveness, transformation, favor, and life, to name a few, can affect the lives of all in radiant ways. On the backdrop of death His radiant colors paint pictures of a brighter world. Christ is on the move in words and deeds and not hanging on a wall for decoration. No such thing as a gorgeous, decorative Christ but a Savior likened to the visual version depicted in the movie *Passion of the Christ* that was viciously beaten for the sake of a devalued world. Resurrection paints a much prettier picture, however, but not in the pictures often found hanging on walls but a view of the world that is enlightened, liberated, and free because of what is depicted on canvas but is yet alive in you and me. While many take note of the iconic cross on the walls of homes, church buildings, museums, and such, while others relish its appearance when placed in brilliant array as fashion statements around the necks of both men and women, this is but an emblem whose true meaning is better served when worn on the inside, within the heart of a theist. In all of His splendor, with hearts filled with the souls of theists from all walks of life filled with His power, the positive God-Talker is not sitting somewhere afar off in an ivory tower, but vigorously passing out John 3:16 invitations on well-traveled streets along with others. As ugly as Golgotha's Hill must have been and as pretty as artists may paint an image of the Savior, His likeness is best captured in real life on the backdrop of death bringing forth living portraits in human beings like you and me—the positive "God-Talkers" of our time.

The question arises, How do you and I fit in this picture? Are you and I Christians or something else? Let's further refine our definition of just who fits the profile. Christians are those who are actively involved in the soul-winning enterprise of spreading His colors and participating in assisting them to flow into a devalued world. Why? So others can be enlightened and involved. The goal is to engage others to become imitators of Christ and be so moved to cross the bridge of natural belief to spiritual belief. There is a big difference in the two. Natural belief is when one drinks water from the faucet believing it's safe, driving your car and trusting that the brakes will work, following the doctor's advice by taking medicine and going under the knife believing healing will come. Natural belief is also going to school hoping that being educated will insure a great future. Yet natural belief is often questionable and not always reliable—even temporal or time-based. The water may be unsafe if contaminated, car brakes will give out with wear and tear, doctors may unintentionally misdiagnose the case or prescribe the wrong medicine, and being educated does not always translate into great employment.

Conversely, spiritual belief is infinite and much more reliable. It's supernatural, solid, and unshakable in its assurance and based on the works and words of the Savior. Thus, it behooves the one Christ carries in the midnight to invite Christ out of the picture frame for a living adventure, taking Him into the marketplace so that others may also witness the power of spiritual belief. You and I may then offer the world an opportunity to experience His characteristic of compassion, armed with a testimony that speaks to His divine intervention in human and spiritual affairs, flowing from the inside out. Armed with spiritual fortitude, you and I will go out into the street and share the knowledge of Him and the power of His acts. This allows others to benefit from a Savior who moves out of pictures and into minds, hearts, and souls producing safe passageways in life.

Paint a picture and hang it on the wall of a devalued world where onlookers can see the masterful portrait of a sinner saved by grace in motion. Display a life which is full of promise with the guarantee of a Christ's preferred future.

700 Left-Handed Believers in Christ
"Being left-handed is a good thing"

The Overcomer was the theme of the résumé. Upon reading the document from page to page, a thread of overcoming insurmountable odds was the theme that leaped from the printed pages. The overcomer has credentials that tell the reader Heaven has the last word for a lover of Christ and speaks to the disbelievers of a devalued world, the message being that it's not where a sinner washed in His blood starts that determines the end but the insight that is gained which writes volumes on the manuscript of the convert's future. This is accomplished when a left-handed worldview is used to tell of the special skills that can be gained from encountering and experiencing the works and words of the Christ on a personal and spiritual realm. This worldview depicts the importance of focusing on inner growth and development, which blesses the one possessing this worldview and provides a better pathway on which to travel for others who otherwise would be journeying down a dead-end street. This viewpoint is fueled by an inner strength that comes from the heavens and combats the right-handed worldview that results in living below the snake line. The snake line is an invisible line of elevation. Above the snake line Satan cannot poison the warriors who are fighting the good fight of faith with the venom of doubt and pessimism. Christ calls the "God-Talkers" to rise above the snake line where the atmosphere is conducive to positive change, the potential to be and to become an agent used by the heavens to assist those who may be stranded on the side of the road. Above the snake line there is growth and progress; below the snake line is decay and regression. Above the snake line is where dreams and hopes flourish; below the snake line there are no green pastures or fragrant fields of flowers. Above the snake line the spirit man reaches for the heavens and enjoys the benefits of being a resident alien; below the snake line the poisonous loud noises and infiltration of negativity and chaos of a Godless generation are causing death on dead-end streets.

In the life of a soldier and trooper of heaven, somewhere between spiritual belief and disbelief, doubts surface their ugly heads and are great enemies to a left-handed worldview. Doubt in Christian combatants' abilities to have achievements and accomplishments are dampened by a right-handed worldview, which speaks to outer vestments of status, money, survival-of-the-fittest mindset and personal influence in high worldly places. Bookmarks of a right-handed worldview outline chapter after chapter of defeated persons living below the snake line with little hope of a better day. Sad outcomes and hopelessness from a litany of heartbreaking after heartbreaking statistics paint a portrait of the reign of darkness with no light in sight. On the surface doubt gives the allusion that an uncertain tomorrow will remain uncertain. Because of this type of worldview below the snake line, statistics like the following would be impossible to overcome. For instance, 1 out of 4 youth of this day are contracting the virus that causes AIDS; 1/4 of kids under 18 in the world have not had a clean glass of water; 60 percent of children are born by single mothers; there are 1.4 million gang members across the land—the highest since 2009; 67 percent of young Black men who attend college do not graduate and 288,000 young people of color dropped out of high school in 2012. Compounding these thoughts, our judicial system has added some bad apples to this mixed bag of degradation that further contribute to the chaos below the snake line. A particular judge who sat upon the bench was sentenced to 28 years in prison. He had been paid 2.5 million dollars for sending over 4,000 under-privileged youth to a private prison. This kind of abuse of power is criminal and disheartening. Yet screaming from a nearby street above the snake line is an overcomer of the poison of Satan hollering that the judge's obvious right-handed worldview is not the only way to travel.

Putting so much credence into outerwear, in keeping with a right-handed worldview, leads to an emptiness/nothingness that is void of inner peace and purpose. The glamorization of me, myself, and I only leads to more degradation in an already doubting world. As the overcomer of the poison of Satan screams come from above the snake line fall on ears and lives in search of a message that pierces the right-handed worldview, changing the viewpoint to one of glorifying God, the Christ, and a spiritual belief that transcends the mundane world. This sojourner is now found reaching for the Hand that pulls people out of the physical into the spiritual, causing a new lease on life.

The screaming from a nearby street by another overcomer of Satan's fatal toxic fumes, who has witnessed life above the snake line, continues declaring that solace, strength, and substance can be gained from discovering the Savior on the street less traveled and a left-handed worldview is a much better choice to make in a devalued world. Christ's words and works can and will change a right-handed worldview upside down. This happens as hope, faith, and love turn cursing into blessings and the invisible line is crossed into the spiritual realm of the impossible being possible. The overcomer of the enemies of venom is constantly faced with the battle that has to be waged in order to gain the inward skills required to combat a right-handed worldview. On every street are reminders that defeat will be the end result with the spiritual approach. Not adhering to the descriptions given by doubters, like-minded conquers strive for a new reality that is based on the words and works of Him who is still providing signs and wonders in a world riddled with pessimism. Inner strength is gained by allowing His words and works to combat doubt and build an unwavering foundation built on His promises upon which to stand. What the right-handed worldview calls weak, in a left-handed worldview the Presence of the Christ makes strong.

Armed with inner fortitude gained from this "Spiritual Formation," the left-handed fighter of the throne has skills to fight the good fight. Strength is gained from growth and development from the inside out, caused by focusing on the inward being/inward self—having the spiritual exercises of prayer, fasting, study of the scriptures, praise, and worship. From Spiritual Formation births optimism and from optimism births skill and from skill births spiritual victories against the enemy of doubt.

The Holy Bible speaks of the 700 left-handed warriors who the world counted out. It was a right-handed worldview account, which chronicled that their left-handedness made them lame, disabled, ineffective, and unconvincing warriors. According to their worldly point of view the left-handedness made them unable to achieve victory. But with God, they were made able and contributed greatly to victory because of their special skills (Judges 20). It was because of their skill with a bow and ability to hurl stones at the enemy with great accuracy, that victory was won by David's army. Against great numbers they were victorious. The warrior's skill comes from the ability to overcome in spite of being left-handed in a right-handed world. Nothing and no one can impede, hinder, or bind Christ's soldier especially when Spiritual Formation is always on the agenda. Conforming to the image of Christ as a direct result of wearing Him in the inside translates to the Glory of God and the abundance of the heavens shining forth through the world of the fighter of Heaven. Thus, he or she is one who conquers doubt brought on by a world filled with doubters who have yet to be skilled in the spiritual exercises of prayer, fasting, study of the scriptures, praise, and worship. Believing what the Christ believed, loving like the Christ loved, and possessing the character that the Christ exhibited gives the warrior faith to overcome doubt. The outward threats, pressures, and warnings on the street of the mind, heart, and soul have to be removed. As slacking from spiritual exercises and weakness of faith are replaced with determination to train in the spirit realm and lean on the Savior for aid, the warrior becomes an overcomer. The great foe of pessimism is no match for the victorious ones from the army of Christ who excels in the process of allowing the words and works of Christ and spiritual agencies from above to take shape and form the skills required on the inside to fight and win against the enemy of Satan, although he continues day after day to hurl stones of doubt into the theist's world. The active process of engaging in spiritual exercises as part of the "God-Talkers" world is the continuing goal to strive to reach and change a generation who appear to be drowning in the sea of doubt below the snake line.

CLEAR THE AIR BELIEF IN CHRIST
"Justice is color-blind"

When the smoke settles and gases form in the atmosphere, spiritual breathing becomes difficult below the snake line. Mortal lungs then must work harder to inhale and then exhale. Unfortunately, the climate is not conducive to an inner respiratory system to function at optimum level let alone any level worth noting. It becomes increasingly problematic for Heaven's oxygen to reach important organs for the body for which Christ paid so much to function. Suffocating on fumes begins the cycle to the end of abundant life as we know it and unless the spiritual vacuum sucks out the impurities in the air, breathing slows down until the last breath is taken.

These words describe life lived below the snake line as individuals seek to breathe air that is contaminated by the smoke and gases the "Prince of the Air" has dispersed in the atmosphere. The reality to such a scenario is gripping to say the least. It is no secret the Christians and the Great Cloud of Witnesses have been here before—a place of no pastures and dead-ended streets—breathing unhealthy air in need of spiritual Febreze to be cast into the environment, not to mask the air but to purify the air so that the opportunity for a better breathing experience can take place. Every person in the universe deserves this air that breeds green grass and pristine lighted avenues. I watched and listened with these thoughts in mind to a moving commentary by Martin Bashir on the death of Black teenager Trayvon Martin and the subsequent Zimmerman not-guilty verdict rendered in the case. Upon hearing his words, several meaningful beliefs came to my mind.

- First, it is a big mistake to write a Child of Christ out of the story until the end has been written.
- Secondly, the fight for social justice and equality is an unending fight in the natural realm.

- Thirdly, it is a big mistake to write people who live in a devalued world out of the picture when the spraying of spiritual Febreze on their lives will allow them to pass through the process of individuation.
- Fourthly, individuation is the process one goes through on the path of becoming whole in mind, heart, and soul, and given better air to inhale and exhale can lift them above the snake line. Christ's words and works pull out the impurities from damaged lungs, causing healing and wholeness to be the result and gaining spiritual lungs to run the race to the very end.
- But, more importantly and fifthly, individuation—the process one goes through to becoming whole in mind, heart, and soul, is the vacuum needed to suck out the impurities in the air. The extracting out of the impurities in the air and the opportunity to excel is the order of the day.
- And, finally my son (Gerald II) along with so many others fathers and sons are looking for social justice and sometimes couldn't find any on the natural scene.

These six thoughts were gleaned that faithful day Martin Bashir on "Clear the Air" told the story of Trayvon Martin the young teenager who was killed by George Zimmerman. Martin Bashir said,

> Stories are now being carefully fed to certain sections of the media — that he (Martin) was suspended from school after his bag was found to contain marijuana residue. That he once wrote graffiti on school grounds…wow! And, to top it all, the greatest act of social criminality for a kid of color—that he may have had a gold tooth. Wow! Call the police. Even if these petty incidents were true, what on earth do they have to do with the fact that George Zimmerman chose to kill him? But, let's compare Trayvon Martin with the history of another man; only this one committed some real offenses and all of them after his 17th birthday. When this individual was 20, he was arrested for disorderly conduct after he got drunk and stole a Christmas wreath from a hotel.
> So that's drunk, disorderly and theft. When he was 26, he took his 16-year-old brother on an underage drinking spree. He lost control of his car, hitting a garbage can but continued driving. When he was 30, he was arrested and found guilty of driving under the influence of alcohol.

His driving license was suspended for two years, even though his friends tried to say that it was just for 30 days. Does this brief history make him a social wretch; a criminal with no regard for other road users; a drunk, a disgraceful influence upon young people, including his own 16-year-old brother? What do you want to call him? Scum of the earth; hoodlum; criminal? In fact, America ended up calling him the 43rd President of the United States—George W. Bush.[4]

As his comments went forth one could only hold their breath and with anticipation await his next words. Part of his 3-minute-and-39-second segment tells how Trayvon didn't get the chance to go through the process of individuation. The new air Christ brings is that any and everyone who accepts the John 3:16 Invitation can hit a home run in the game of life.

Trayvon's story is moving, hurting, and sad to say the least and he was not afforded the chance to become the next CEO of a Fortune 500 Company, owner of multiple Starbucks or McDonald stores or a Telecommunication Mogul, or the next President of Morehouse College or Ohio State University. The most humble beginning is the formula for His air of individuation change from life below the snake line to above the snake line is available to the least, left out, and last in. Our 43rd President George Bush had the opportunity to grow, mature, and achieve because of this term "individuation." He was allowed to grow out of behavior unbecoming a person seeking to make a difference in a society where people have trouble breathing below the snake line. He could go down streets, which would otherwise be closed off because of barriers put up to keep unwanted persons out who desire to live above the snake line. He was allowed to glow with achievements and accomplishments that would not have been witnessed by others because of the chances afforded him above the snake line. The Christ is still cruising down dead-end streets spraying spiritual Febreze upon the lifeless, transforming them into new Disciples of Christ. A Savior who is no respecter of persons and an equal-opportunity Christ is looking, stopping, reaching, and waiting for anyone with a short or long rap sheet—"come see a man," as did the Samaritan woman at the well—and witness His Signs and Wonders.

My son and so many others were looking for justice in the natural realm and didn't find it. Trayvon was robbed of the opportunity to make a significant contribution below and above the snake line. He was victim of a society that was ready to throw him away, but a Savior was prepared to take this young man into His flock. Gerald II, with tears in his eyes and a broken spirit, wanted answers for this injustice. Looking to the One who dispenses justice in both realms, I offered my son consolation in the spiritual realm when little was afforded in the natural realm. Christ never promised that there would not be injustices in this devalued world but what He did promise was that He'd be with me and my son in the midst of an unjust world, Martin Bashir concluded his commentary by saying:

> So, while you may be tempted to divert your attention from what really happened to Trayvon Martin, here are the only three facts that really matter:
>
> *First:* A man with a gun chose to pursue an unarmed teenager who had done nothing wrong.
>
> *Second:* The man with the gun chose to initiate a confrontation with the teenager, after he was advised not to.
>
> *Third:* As a result of the confrontation, the man with the gun shot the teenager to death. And when you focus on the facts, it's not the color of his teeth that keep coming back to haunt you, it's the color of his skin.[5]

Heaven is always watching and will turn injustices into justice in the end. Although we fight for social justice and equality on this side of the Jordan, Judgment day is what I told my son is coming and Trayvon and others like him will get justice, for God will not be made out of a lie. Heaven will not stand for this and the perpetrator should beware of reaping what one sows. The workers of Christ then must concentrate on being agriculturally and architecturally sound as it relates to the process of individuation. If on the natural realm no justice will be found, on the spiritual realm God will surly pass down judgment. However, we must be rooted and grounded in what is right and morally correct and build a foundation with walls and rooms that have the spiritual air of the Throne running through the ventilation system. It is Heaven's position to make Justice roll down the streets of this world and the "God-Talkers" position is to be on the right side of Justice when the Ultimate Judge passes down the sentences. I saw my son's countenance improve as he felt reassured that the opportunity to have life above the snake line was still his to experience along with so many others across the land, and the remaining George Zimmermans of the world will have to deal with a Just Christ who died for all.

Impossible Odds Belief in Christ
"Can't count us out"

It has been said that the making of a Christian believer is the direct result of "the sum total of their experiences." When I was six years old, I was hit by a car; at 14, I cut a major vein in the left arm and almost bled to death; and at 22 years old, two weeks before my trial sermon, the furnace at home blew up in my face, and I was told I might never see again. Being written out of life by onlookers who declared he'd never get out of High School and would be in prison before turning 25, Christ's words and works changed the odds. At my baptism into the Heavenly Crew, the odds-makers in hell predicted the probability of success in the kingdom enterprise. Odds were set, but not in my favor of crossing the finish line and hearing God declare my faithfulness for putting into practice His words and works. On the contrary, the odds are set against me as hell bet against my traveling down the street called "Right." Every detour, road block, traffic jam, accident, distraction, road rage, uneven road, closed lanes, and obstacle imaginable would be thrown in the path to keep me from making it to the 12 gates of the City. Yes, hell's odds-makers are still betting against this "God-Talker"—that he will not to be able to win against the wiles of the devil. Here are some of the odds that are being waged against all who give the preacher their hand and the Lord their hearts:

1 out of 1 trillion are the odds of a promiscuous person being faithful to a woman/man.

1 out of 100 million are the odds of a liar to tell the truth.

1 out of 1 billion are the odds preachers will not commit the six deadly sins of preaching as described by Lucy Lind Hogan and Robert Stephen Reid:
- The Pretender (The Problem of In-authenticity)
- The Egoist (The Problem of Self-absorption)
- The Manipulator (The Problem of Greediness)
- The Panderer (The Problem of Trendiness)
- The Crusader (The Problem of Exploitation)
- The Demagogue (The Problem of Self-righteousness)[6]

1 out of 77 million "God-Talkers" will not conquer or defeat the seven deadly sins of the House of God— wrath, greed, sloth, pride, lust, envy, and gluttony.

1 out of 370 thousand Congregations will allow the Holy Spirit to have His way.

1 out of 106 million will walk from homosexual/lesbian/bisexual lifestyles.

1 out of 100 million will win against drug and alcohol addictions.

1 out of 100 million will praise and worship God in spirit and truth.

1 out of 7 billion will witness to His goodness below and above the snake line.

1 out of 700 million will be Churches without Walls.

And the list goes on and on…

0 out of 500 million will bring a soul to Christ.

0 out of 700 million will use God given talents and God given gifts to Glorify Him.

0 out of 3 billion will fight for justice for all people.

0 out of 5 trillion will turn in outer vestments for inner vestments.

> 0 out of 3 trillion will practice the I*nsanity of Theology*—promoting an ongoing belief and faith in God to turn situations around for the betterment of the individual, the Church, and the community, even when the evidence points to the impossible.

The odds are not in believer's favor. But wait and ask the fat lady not to warm up in her dressing room. You and I do not have to fight against the odds alone, especially with Him who is the only One to overcome the grave. We have overcome greater odds than these with Him who has never lost against the odds. Hell waged against Him getting out of the grave at

0 out of 100,000,000,000 to the 8 billionth power.

And what did heaven do with this odd that came from the books from hell? Heaven watched as God busted Him out of the grave and He rose with all power in His hand. Nothing is impossible in and with Heaven and what will always be important to the Christian, community, and the Church is that no odds are too great for His words and works to overcome. With all of Heaven's resources victory can be won against any odds. No matter how dark the night, Heaven can shine light on the backdrop of death. Christ's words and works do their best work in the darkest of night. Just ask Jessica Buchanan. Her story that seems it could only come from a Hollywood movie script. She writes:

> The attack begins as if an umpire has just blown a starting whistle. A large car roars up beside us and careens to a stop, splashing mud all over our windows. Men with AK-47s encircle our car, pounding on the doors, shouting over each other in Somali. Their behavior is ferocious. My heart goes straight to my throat. Adrenaline sends a jolt of fear from head to toe. The terror feels like heat, like we are suddenly being roasted alive inside this car. My brain is seizing up from trying to process this. I hear a little version of my voice in the back of my skull chanting: This is very bad, this is very bad, this is very bad.[7]

What were the odds she would be rescued in real life and brought back from death? On that chilly night in January of 2012, President Obama made the call to send in the unstoppable Seal Team 6, the unstoppable military force that strikes fear into the heart of evildoers, to rescue Jessica Buchanan from kidnappers in Somalia. Our 44th President sent in the best team at his disposal to rescue this young woman who was truly at the end of her rope. Praying, pleading, and petitioning the throne of God over and over and over again asking for freedom from these men who held her hostage. From days that turned into weeks and weeks that turned into months calling on the One who is always listening to the cry of His children. Then in the still of the night Seal Team 6 descended from the air, killed her kidnappers, and rescued her from her captives. As she was giving an interview to a reporter, Jessica told of the impossible escape and a chilling description as she was in the care of Seal Team 6. As they were making their escape they told her to get down. As she was lying down on the ground each member of the team covered her until the danger subsided. Then on to the Ronda view point for extraction. The nameless Seal Team 6 accomplished the impossible. Wow! What a story that against the odds Jessica was saved.

Deeper in the isles of time this is nothing new to the greatest of all Seal Team Leaders. Angels of Heaven have been doing the same thing for those lost souls in the natural and the spiritual realm across the annals of time. They've been rescuing the lost, fearful captives of the enemy since God breathed into the first Adam's spiritual lungs. The Christ is more than an unstoppable military force but is an unstoppable spiritual force at the disposal of a God who continues to do the impossible every day—setting captives free and declaring this is the acceptable year of favor. Armed with His words and works, He is raising the "God-Talker" from the gutters of impossible situations when they are at the end of their natural and spiritual ropes. Since Heaven has a multiplicity of ways to rescue, revive, and restore seekers who are looking for a way out of dead-end boulevards, stagnant traffic on closed roads and strugglers on clogged thoroughfares, the Christian theist places signs that lead to stable avenues—those that are with marked signs saying nothing is too hard on a street called "Christ's Drive of Endless Possibilities."

God-Talker's Anthem
"'Tis so sweet"

Praise God I have not been led astray with regard to the thought, "Not wanting to exist but wanting to live." To live at times is more than a challenge and can be bittersweet to say the least. It is as if life is a two-sided coin with the heads side being happiness and the tail side being sorrow. I'm convinced life can make you bitter or it can make you better, particularly after a great loss, great defeat, or a great downfall. The key to having the right perspective when choosing to face life with the attitude "If life is going to give you lemons choose to make lemonade." It is a choice that must be made. It's easier said than done, you find, when it's your turn to endure hardship.

Louisa M. R. Stead, a "God-Talker," faced the bitter side of life; and mind you it was not because she deserved it or because she caused it. No, no it was because it was her turn to deal with tragedy. According to the story: It was a beautiful sunny day. Louisa M. Stead, her husband, and her daughter, Lily, decided to go for a picnic. They went picnicking on Long Island Sound. While having their picnic, the Steads heard a scream. It was from a young boy. Mr. Stead ran to the rescue. Louisa Stead and young Lily watched helplessly as Mr. Stead and the boy drowned. Their troubles were not over yet, however, and without her husband, Mrs. Stead became very poor and destitute. Yet God never left her. He provided for her always and she and her daughter made it through. Louisa learned to trust God, and thus the words to the song; "'Tis So Sweet to Trust in Jesus" was born. First stanza:

> 'Tis so sweet to trust in Jesus, and to take Him at His Word;
> Just to rest upon His promise,
> And to know, "Thus says the Lord!"[8]

Recently, I played over and over again this song, "'Tis So Sweet to Trust in Jesus," sung by the dismantled soulful Christian group "Commission." Listening to the melody, words, and vocals and reflecting on Louisa M. R. Stead's story,

I wondered what it would take to really trust The Christ when all hell breaks loose. Real trust in the Christ is likened to any occasion when one goes to bed at night believing the bed will hold them up all the night. Consequently, can we trust in Jesus and take Him at His word to be there through the good and the bad, ups and the downs, times of plenty and times of drought. Will we trust Him when we can't see Him or hear Him or feel Him? It all comes down to this—can we trust Him to the point where we are vulnerable, helpless, and susceptible to the trials of this life? But more importantly, will we give Him permission to speak into our lives in our vulnerability? Surely His reputation, character, truth, grace, power, and presence ought to move us into giving ourselves over to Him and allowing the teacher to make us His student. It appears to be a logical and reasonable chance to take, especially when life has thrown the kitchen sink at us. I am reminded of one of my favorite gospel singers, Fred Hammond, and his soulful rendition of this particular stanza of one of the favorite hymns of the Church:

> Jesus, Jesus, how I trust Him! How I've proved Him o'er and o'er;
> Jesus, Jesus, precious Jesus! O for grace to trust Him more!

Even in this writing, I recall how chills traveled down my spine, as all I could think about was that trusting in Christ is not inherent, it is learned. "God-Talkers" learn to trust in Him, learning to prove Him, and learning to lean on Him. With each of life's calamities, there is the potential for learning as He proves ever faithful and up to the task of redeeming us and restoring us. This builds our desire and ability to trust—to trust—Him even more with the next test. And then, when we face those tumultuous predicaments, as did the songwriter Louisa M. R. Stead, we too can sing in the night, "'Tis so sweet to trust in Him because He will never leave us or forsake us."

In the Gospel of John, we come to the conclusion that without Him you cannot make it in this life. The One who draws us closer to conforming to Christ's image takes center stage. And we allow the strength of the Masterful Ghost and the lively movements of the Holy Spirit to work on us from the inside out. Stay on the Potter's table and endure the uncomfortable experience of being made over. Sometimes it will be hurtful, sometimes it will feel pleasant, but all the time His touch is what we all need. Let Him top off our cups to run over and fill our saucers, as long and as many times as it takes to refocus our eyes to see straight, reshape our mouths to speak straightforward, our hands to stay glued to the gospel plow, and our feet ready to run to do His will. Succumb and surrender to His authority, His teaching us to keep looking to the One who died for us. Who is He? He is The Inner Immanuel! The One who can favor us to walk the straight line and walk the walk and talk the talk.

Chapter 3

The Spirit That Aids Drunks Walking Tightrope Wires

THE INNER VESTMENT OF THE HOLY SPIRIT

"The mission of Heaven's Global Positioning System
is to keep us balanced and on course"

And then God came nearer. While being everywhere at the same time, God is yet making Himself assessible to the heavenly God-Talkers in expressions and actions. And then, He moves nearer still. A true follower of Christ decides that a much closer relationship with God is needed and the plan is formulated and executed. Through the womb of a virgin girl, in the presence of a carpenter of wood, outside amongst the farm animals, unaware to the innkeeper He put the "only begotten Son" out of the glorious Kingdom and into the cold. The Lamb of God would be the key to the greatest plan ever to be conceived of in earth and the universe. He came to be the substitute of all substitutes, a surrogate for all who march up the Ugly Hill called Golgotha, as followers of Christ taking up our crosses daily in an equally ugly and sinful world. Such is the exit of The One, "Jesus the Son," and the entrance and the beginning of the reign of The Inner Immanuel. He is the one who becomes the Christian's Guide, Comforter, and Teacher. Think of the magnitude of His love. God who is no longer just for us, God who is no longer with us, but now God is in us. God came to reside in the inner parts of His creation. The Inner Immanuel is the Holy Ghost! He comes under the radar moving into the inner sphere. God invades the center of our human space and takes residence in our Core. He becomes our Alpha Region and begins the process of the continuing process of conforming the believer's inner triune life. So much closer does He move into us to the extent that His breath that was breathed into the nostrils of born-again believers all around the globe has taken up permanent residence in their inner being.

The age of the spiritual turbulence of change and its impact on and in substances other than the terrain is well-documented in the Holy Bible. It comes to bring a much-needed change from having the old Adam's character to walking in the new Adam's likeness. Released from the heavens into the innermost being of the theist, one professing and requesting that Christ become Savior and Lord, He (the Holy Ghost) takes up office. In a lowly, unassuming, and yet powerful way, having the power to tear down the strongholds of Satan and any forces that might come against His people, He builds up divine fortified walls of protection from the darts of Satan. He waits for an invitation to enter. He is as subtle as the wind working through the trees, shifting and changing while invisibly making His presence, power, and dynamic movement seen throughout the circumstances of time. He demonstrates his ability to penetrate walls that have been erected to keep Him out. He hovers overhead and when the invitation is accepted, He takes up residence in the mind, heart, and soul. He becomes God's new and most important way to relate to His positive "God-Talkers." No longer being satisfied to be solely the Creator, and glad to have been with His creation as the Son, now God is ecstatic to move and be inside His creation. Yes, His office is open to the universe and the marquee reads, "He is available for God's business." His business is to transform the "God-Talkers" to the image of Christ. By performing the following services, being the begetter of the new way, God will interact with life, as the life-giver, as the imparter of power, as the eternal comforter and helper, as the teacher of truth, as the remitter of all truth, as the guide of all truth, as the revealer of Christ in events, as the glorifier of Christ, and as the chief witness of Christ. The Inner Immanuel comes to make sure Satan's agenda will not be met as the enemy seeks to disarm the warrior of power, distract the follower of the Trinity from purpose, and disenable Christians from productivity in efforts to destroy their chances for reaching their potential. He will make the way straight that Heaven's agenda of turning the world upside down will occur and heavenly witnesses will be birthed into a world that is thirsty for the Master's Water, which will quench all thirsts.

The Inner Immanuel is the Comforter, Guide, and Teacher of the body of Christ. He brings wisdom, understanding, knowledge, and the fear of the Lord. He brings abundance, gives us the ability to carry out God's will in the earth, instructs into the mysteries of God, makes us better servants of the Most High, and gives sublime rest from the hurts and pains of this life. In the Old Testament and New Testament He was called the "Spirit of God" 378 times, "Holy Spirit" 468 times, and the "Holy Ghost" 385 times. In each instance He is the breath, air, movement, vivacity, vigor, truth, and corrector of God whose works and power propel the souls of the "God-Talker." He is:

- The Inner Immanuel (John 3:6).
- He helps us in worship (John 4:20-24).
- He urges us toward salvation (John 6:44).
- He is our living water (John 7:38).
- He will be with us forever (John 14:16).
- The world at large cannot accept Him (John 14:17).
- He lives with us and in us (John 14:17).

- He teaches us (John 14:26).
- He reminds us of Christ's words (John 14:26; 15:26).
- He convicts us of sin and teaches us right from wrong (John 16:8).
- He guides us into truth and provides insight into future events (John 16:13).
- He gives glory to the Christ (John 16:14).

His three most important tasks are:

1) To convict sins of this world and call for repentance;

2) To be the presence in this world to show heavenly standards of what is right in the eyesight of God for those who are sold out for the kingdom;

3) To prove that Christ and His disciples can conquer Satan and his host of fallen angels.

As the believer advocates, the Spirit of truth serves as the helper, encourager, and strengthener as He points to the teaching, illuminating, and reminding us that He ministers to the mind, heart, and soul. It was the Christ who said of Him,

> "When the Friend I plan to send you from the Father comes—the Spirit of Truth issuing from the Father—he will confirm everything about me. You, too, from your side must give your confirming evidence, since you are in this with me from the start." (John 15:26)

Before He made Himself known to "God-Talkers," in the heavens His reputation is celebrated for being the catalyst of change. Without Him, at best you and I could hope for not faltering, fumbling, and failing the easiest spiritual tasks. As Christians experience more of His presence, power, and dynamic movement, they are transformed into disciples who are not only fans but followers of the One who said He was coming, understanding that He is welcome, as Fred Hammond sings, "Holy Spirit You are welcome in this place, Holy Spirit we submit to Your authority." It is in submitting to the Holy Spirit's authority that the weak flesh of the "God-Talkers" becomes stronger to do the will of the Father in a devalued world. However, Christianity is authenticated when the innate weakness of the flesh is noted and used as an excuse to avail God's grace as a license plate to do one's own thing. Rather you and I seek, strive, and succeed in His power. Submitting to His power can be likened to being drunk with spiritual wine, and as John R. W. Stott provides light upon this problem by giving the example of being infused with His willingness to impact "God-Talker's" lives and the downward spiral of being without the operation of His office. He writes of the difference of being drunk with the wine of this mundane, spiritless, and void existence and the impression the Child of God receives from the works and workings of His actions being played out in a living, vibrant, fresh movement. He says:

> We can indeed agree that in both drunkenness and the fullness of the Spirit two strong influences are at work within us, alcohol in the blood stream, and the Holy Spirit in our hearts. But, whereas excessive alcohol leads to unrestrained and irrational license, transforming the drunkard into an animal, fullness in the spirit leads to restrained and rational moral behavior, transforming the Christian into the image of Christ. Thus, the results of being under the influence of spirits on the one hand and of the Holy Spirit of God on the other are totally and utterly different. One makes us like a beast, the other like Christ.[1]

The goal is always to be spiritually intoxicated and submitting to the Inner Immanuel, who provides much-needed strength in conquering Satan's agenda. You and I will always find drink from Jacob's well and must allow Christ's water to quench the thirst of a thirsty traveler. Moving in step with God's Holy Ghost, spiritual drunkenness is the wine which controls, burns up sin, heals the brokenhearted, leads into all spiritual truth, wipes the tears from their eyes in the midnight hour, rocks the Christian to sleep in the time of crisis, quiets the mind, fills the heart with joy, and is the wind that makes the soul travel down the sea of life. Every day, every hour, every minute, and every second you and I go to the tap of an endless supply which fills the inner parts of our lives and permeates the inner being, causing transformation of ideals, standards, morals, doctrines, behaviors, and lifestyles. The Inner Immanuel empowers the Christian to serve God to the fullest. Dr. John Owens once said,

> The sin of the Old Testament was the rejection of God the Father. The sin of the New Testament was the rejection of God the Son and the sin of this present age is the rejection of God the Holy Spirit.[2]

Positive God-Talkers have to avoid the temptation of going by Calvary to get sins forgiven and not going by Pentecost to receive the power needed for this spiritual journey.

THE GOD-TALKER EMPOWERED BY THE SPIRIT
"The flow"

When the universe is blind to hurting people's pain and deaf to our losses and sorrows, the Inner Immanuel sees and is not silent in His actions. Moving at the speed of light, He steps in when others will step out. From a personal vantage point, allow me to again reference my painful childhood. When the anesthesia wore off, I was lying in a bed of cold water, which was poured on my eyes after the furnace blew up in my face. While lying outside of the specialist's office at Barnes Hospital in St. Louis, I was in severe pain. It was at that point that He stepped in and moved my mother to lean over and recite into my eye the 23rd Psalm. The pain gave way to His presence and He replaced it with calm. Another case in point was some years later during my matriculation as a seminary student when student loans ran out and the United Negro College funds were depleted. I was called in to the office of the Vice President for Financial Services, Mrs. Elizabeth Littlejohn's office at the Interdenominational Theological Center (ITC), and told to pack and go back to East St. Louis. This was in the last semester of my Graduate School journey toward earning the Master of Divinity Degree. But, He stepped in. This time he moved a fellow classmate, friend, and father-figure, Dr. R. L. White, to tell the

Christian theist, "Don't worry, just come by the office on Thursday and I'll have the $1,500 dollars so you can graduate." And still another case in point, when the theist's mother went on to glory, and not having a biological father to go to, my adopted father, the late Dr. John H. Rouse, was present to hold my hand as one of my very indifferent professors commented, "I don't care about your mother dying, if you don't have my exegeses paper in on time I will fail your ass." He moved, moving his best friend, encourager, and lifelong support Jane Jelks Jones to take up the slack. She aided in carrying this "God-Talker" across the graduation line and raising this positive God-Talker along with her son Ken.

The Inner Immanuel moves through the trees and in the wind, making Him perceive our pain and hear our sorrows to the extent that He will not leave me stranded all alone to face a devalued world. His power is evidenced by actions which speak louder than any words but they bring alive His words and works in this present age. The question surfaces, What does the Holy Ghost do for inner attacks? Anesthesia wears off, Dr. White coming to the rescue is a warm memory, and Jane being the mother to the motherless is a life-long pursuit. The greatest acts of the Holy Ghost's power are performed inside the inner being by allowing His power to get me off the spiritual merry-go-round of sin. Let's take as an example "Electricity." Electricity lights up our homes, cooks our food, and powers our computers, television sets, and other electronic devices. Electricity from batteries keeps our cars running, causes our pacemakers to tick, and makes our flashlights shine in the dark. We've become dependent and reliant upon its presence and power that without it many of us could not adjust nor live. Consider, in 1660 Otto Von Guericke, who was credited with making the second major breakthrough in the history of electricity. His work proved certain objects were electrical insulators (do not allow electricity to flow through). Other objects he found were electrical conductors (allow electricity to flow through). In the natural realm certain objects can be used to block the flow of electricity (electrical insulators), and others will let the flow of electricity move with freedom to reach desired outcomes (electrical conductors). Since the Inner Immanuel can be quenched, the Christian has a decision to make: Be an electrical insulator or be an electrical conductor. The spiritual merry-go-round is nothing more than an electrical insulator that will prevent the Inner Immanuel from carrying out His mission in a believer's life. Continuing to sin (missing the mark), using God's grace as an license to do your own thing or whatever is right in my own eye, will result in rerouting the Power of Heaven from flowing freely to be the empowerment of God—Christ sent by Him into our minds, hearts, and souls to perform. Going around and around looking for a fleshly diversion on the sin ride will cause the Holy Ghost to seek residence elsewhere. And, when it's time to be a witness, to perform a spiritual task and be the salt of the earth and a light on a hill, the Christian could find that the power source has been cut off due to the spiritual insulator of sin. There comes a time in every born-again Christian's life when a decision must be made, a covenant has to made, and a contract signed in agreement with the heavens. The decision has to be final to either deny and suppress the power of the Inner Immanuel which transforms and conforms you and me into the image of Christ, or to be a conductor of the power of the Inner Immanuel to be a witness, perform spiritual tasks, and be the salt of the earth and a light in dark places. Getting off the spiritual merry-go-round of sin will require more than will power; it will require Holy Ghost power! When the decision is made not to be a spiritual insulator and to be and persist in being a spiritual conductor, admitting the weakness of the flesh and making the commitment of relying on the ultimate power of the universe will accomplish getting off the spiritual merry-go-round of sin. This is not natural electricity but spiritual power. The Holy Ghost!

In 1750 Benjamin Franklin pushed the envelope further than he'd ever done before by publishing a proposal for an experiment to prove that lightning is electricity by flying a kite in a storm. On that stormy day in 1752 Ben was not hindered, stopped, or stumped, even though two of his friends had already been electrocuted. Therefore, Ben, not fearing electrocution because of a more compelling feeling that he had the missing component to harness this great power, he raised his kite with a key tied near his hand. When lightning struck the kite, it transferred and was conducted through the key. This proved that lightning was in fact a type of electrical power. Ben felt the electric shock go through his entire body. The first thing I gleaned from this episode in the discovery of electricity is that if one does not have the right key to harness the power of electricity the end result will be falling, faltering, and a literal fiasco. The key to feeling the flow of the Inner Immanuel going through my mind, heart, and soul is getting off the merry-go-round of sin. Sin will not cause one to be spiritually electrocuted where death is the end result. Spiritual death. To be and become the transferred or conducted source in a devalued world is to stay filled with Holy Ghost power and be less filled with the wine of this world and more filled with the spiritual wine of Heaven. Spiritual life will be our reward.

The second thing I gleaned from this episode in the discovery of electricity is that without its conductors providing the avenue for the power to flow, darkness and theological blindness would be the end result. I'm in darkness with no oil to refill the lamp of life, needing assistance by the Spirit to burn out sin and give light to see the Christ. He is the oil that provides the energy to keep the conductor flowing and the lamp filled to give off light, void of light needing the Inner Immanuel to give the light needed to enlighten the mind, heart, and soul. Shedding light that works through positive God-Talkers that performs spiritual tasks, witnessing concerning the actions of God, Christ and the Inner Immanuel will flow in a dark and devalued world.

Deep down where the greatest attack is being waged between good versus evil the action now moves to the outer realm of religion versus inner relationship. Receive the power to move from religious practice that is for outer show to relationship that comes from being willing to grow in His grace. When the lights are off and the cameras stop rolling, religion will not aid you and me with having a relationship with the Inner Immanuel. It is important to note that inner religion is based on inner realities and not outer shows. A religion that moves from the outside in instead of the inside out has little value. A relationship with the Trinity hinges on movement from the inside out and guarantees aid in the light and in the dark. When the hypocrite acting in the sacred halls of Church buildings and worship settings moves out into real life external or surface acts of religion, he cannot make a passing grade with Heaven, as his/her behavior has no discernible relationship with Christ. The attack of SIN is where the struggle is the strongest calling for strength to get off the spiritual merry-go-round of outer religion and where stepping into a powerful inner relationship with God Almighty becomes vital! Bear in mind that there is also inherent evil that lives in the inner parts of the positive "God-Talker," as the Apostle Paul attests to, and there is an ongoing struggle within that goes against the Law of God. It is our inborn Sin nature that separates us from God. Sin is the wall that keeps us from God. Sin is the wrong doing of the Christian and in the Hebrew text has five meanings. They are:

1) missing
2) transgression
3) perversion
4) evil in disposition
5) impiety.

Sin in the Greek text has seven meanings:
1) missing the mark
2) transgression
3) unrighteousness
4) impiety
5) contempt and violation of love
6) depravity
7) lust

On closer investigation of SIN, you and I must confess that our nature is sinful and requires a God whose Laws are holy, just, good, and spiritual to transform our sinfulness to conform us into the image of the Christ. If justice had his way, you and I would be convicted and sentenced to death because of the sin that the Hebrew and Greek words reveal. Grace beseeches the throne and asks God Almighty to give you and me what we do not deserve—pardon from sin—and give us what is really needed—deliverance from SIN along with the other spiritual actions the Inner Immanuel performs. The Inner Immanuel leads you and me to the source of deliverance, Grace *(God's resources at Christ's Expense)*. The incredible thing about Grace is best described as such:

> Longfellow could take a worthless sheet of paper, write a poem on it and make it worth $6,000—that's genius. Rockefeller could sign his name to a piece of paper and make it worth a million dollars—that's capital. Uncle Sam can take a gold coin, stamp an eagle on it and make it worth $20—that's money. A mechanic can take material that is worth $5 and make it worth $50—that's skill. An artist can take a $.50 piece of canvas, paint a picture on it and make it worth $100—that's art. God can take a worthless, sinful life wash it in the blood of Christ, put His Spirit in it and make it a blessing to humanity—that's Grace.[3]

Yes, the Inner Immanuel turns the sinner into a saint, moving from outer shows of religion to inner empowered relationship by putting on the inside a code of honor that seeks to continue to allow Grace to make the blind to see. However, understand that you and I cannot be above sin, but have to deal with sin constructively with the aid of the Spirit. The right relationship with the Trinity assures victory in the struggle of sin. The inward conflict will never cease until the last breath is breathed. Furthermore, until our last breath is taken He must continue to breathe the Breath of God into our spiritual lungs. With the spiritual oxygen gained, the struggle against sin (which is missing the mark of the standards God has set forth in the Holy Bible) is won. Our struggle is between good versus evil and moving from outer religion to inner relationship. Praise God for grace and aid in the spiritual tussle, knowing that the struggle is real and ever present. The Christian is not exempt from struggling with a proud look, a lying tongue, hands that shed innocent blood, and a heart that devises wicked imaginations, feet that are swift in running to mischief, a false witness that speaks lies, and one who soweth discord among the brethren. We must be shrewd in struggling with sexual sins, the spirit of revenge, and the killer of every Christian, community, and Church, the spirit of arrogance. The enemy appeals to the attraction of outer religion which breed's arrogance. But, it is the power of our inner powerful relationship that births humility. Arrogance is the kryptonite that robs positive "God-Talkers" of the real source of power. Arrogance is the enemy that lurks within me. While by definition, arrogance is an insulting way of thinking or behaving that comes from believing that one is better, smarter, or more important than other people; be aware that beyond the definition one cannot fight against such powerful foes alone. The carnal Christian was sold into sin; arrogance and outer religion hold him captive. But, when the Inner Immanuel came to dwell in the inner parts, this changed the shift in the spiritual atmosphere, producing inner relationship with the Slayer of hell. The new Christian received power to fight the old theist nature. The struggle within took on a different light in regard to losing to the old man. The old nature had to yield to the presence, power, and dynamic movement of the Force from the throne. Self-determination and will power had to take a back seat to Holy Ghost power, and the wretched man became infused with the force to fight and win against the penalty and power of sin. The Inner Immanuel gave the Christian the power to win against sin, and when you and I walk in the power of Him, the struggle is not a struggle ending in defeat any longer. Greater is the Inner Immanuel, moving with vivacity, vigor, and victory in the struggles of the "God-Talker," causing an inner conqueror to be born, belief and faith to be strengthened, and a spiritual walk to be energized. The Christian is forever in the debt of the One that moves in the inner being of the mind, heart, and soul, producing the force of good in the name of the Kingdom through having relationship with the Trinity.

THE SIDE EFFECTS OF BEING EMPOWERED BY THE SPIRIT
"We want His side effects"

Side Effects—the term readily denotes something alternative to a positive occurrence in the physical activity of a person or thing—a cause and response relationship, if you will. More often than not, varying levels of side effects can be associated with the ingestion of different products in the physical body. We cite for consideration pharmaceutical drugs, the consumption of alcoholic beverages, the illegal use of and withdrawal from recreational drugs, even eating some foods that may deliver more negative than complementary reactions to normal healthy activity. But let us turn our attention first to the lyrics of the song the "Side Effects of You," by popular songstress Fantasia, for a moving rendition of a personal story. Hopefully it supports the first level of our thesis and understanding of the incomparable side effects of being empowered by the ultimate power, the Holy Spirit. We find the artist Fantasia singing about a relationship and her hope that a man could cure her of loneliness and keep her stable throughout this life. However, as the story unfolds we find that being with him didn't help her loneliness but made it worse. He was supposed to take away the pain and take care of her but instead she can't breathe and finds herself losing balance, falling down, and having sleepless nights whenever he's around. The side effects for her were these things that happen when he is in her life.

Moving on to the second level we go from the emotional imbalance and disparity of a dysfunctional relationship and continue our discovery in the realm of human body illnesses. As human beings, getting older by all accounts, visibly, neurologically, and physically the body begins to deteriorate or break down. On consultation and examination by a physician, a specialist trained to treat illnesses that arise in this life cycle often prescribes medicine. It seems as if pharmaceutical companies are more interested in treating the symptoms of a disease than in coming up with a cure for said diseases. Billions of dollars are spent on the symptoms and not the cure. Depending on the illness/disease a medication will be given to treat the problem and hopefully give the patient the desired result. For instance, there is a medication that can be prescribed for persons who have psoriasis of the skin, rheumatoid arthritis, and psoriatic arthritis. The great thing concerning this drug is that it works. The spotted skin of psoriasis heals and the sufferers of this unsightly skin problem no longer have to be ashamed of having spots and trying whatever methods they can derive to hide them in public or in private. But, before we shout with joy about the help this medication delivers to its patients, let us also consider its side effects that bring to light yet another problem. While one will have clear skin the side effects of this drug may outweigh the benefits. These side effects can be defined as "an often harmful and unwanted effect of the drug or chemical that occurs along with the desired effect: a result of an action that is not expected or intended." While the medication delivers on its intent to provide clear and unblemished skin, the side effects can produce any of the following: risk of infection, risk of cancer, Hepatitis B infection, nervous system problems, blood problems, and heart failure. Wow! Side effects are a serious matter that every person who takes a prescribed drug must be aware of.

Now, let's move to the heart of our thesis and the third level of side effects that are the consequences of sin. Consider this scenario. I was burning the candle at both ends—working all-day and most of the night. I was a lifeguard at Lincoln Swimming Pool by day and a floor guard at the M. L. King Skating Rink by night. It was at the swimming pool during that fateful summer of 1980 when the Lifeguard of humankind saved me from the pool of sin. The sun was bright that day and the water looked different for some reason. All eight lifeguards on duty were looking for love in all the wrong places. The life of sin was taking its toll on my psyche and the search was on for a remedy from the emptiness, restlessness, and guilt. The disease is sin and I was hoping to cure it with the presence of a young woman. Then out of nowhere a solution presented itself. One of the eight lifeguards met the Greatest of all Lifeguards (Christ) in the fall of 1979 and came to work that summer of 1980. He was a new "God-Talker" preaching the gospel. Here was another Christian who had taken the prescription for the same illness I had been suffering from. The heaviness of sin had weighed me down and was affecting my physical body—I had burning whenever I urinated and discharge in my underwear. The symptoms got worse that day when Pop Myles called all his lifeguards to the deep end of the pool for training. One by one he told us to get from under a towel and into the water. Then he pulled a 25-pound brick block and tossed it into the water. He made us all go to the bottom of a 10-foot pool to retrieve the 25-pound brick block. I went down to retrieve this weight from the bottom of the pool. No matter how hard I tried I could not get the brick to the bank of the pool. None of us could get it done. To add to the struggle of Pop Myles's demand, my symptoms got worse while using the men's room. "What is wrong with me?" I asked my teammate. He said, "You need penicillin to clear up that STD. Go to the clinic, and they will prescribe what you need. Just follow the prescription and you will be healed." Deeper into the episode the real sickness raised its ugly head. "You keep sharing with us concerning your experience with God, Jesus, and the Holy Spirit. Can they help me with my emptiness, restlessness, and guilt?" I asked. He replied, "Yes, they can help you with the sin and the side effects of sin."

The universe is infinite, chaotic, and cold and the cosmic question is, "Who can aid humankind with sin and the side effects of sin?" The fourth possible level could move to the positive acts of the Inner Immanuel to get another new "God-Talker" to answer the call to change the world around them. Since sin can be likened to attempting to pull a 25-pound brick weight from the bottom of a 10-foot pool where no one could get it to the bank. And, as one goes into a place seeking rest, sin will not permit you to find green pastures. Looking for a way and seeking relief, the Inner Immanuel aids you and me to experience warmth from the heavens. His special endowment of power counteracts the negativity found in the universe resulting in the production of the positive force required for the "God-Talker" to walk the straight line. The chains of sin that weigh me down are dropped. The Inner Immanuel brings with Him His indwelling and infilling presence that combats all the negative forces of sin and neutralizes sin's side effects. Consequently, He brings His side effects that cure the symptoms of emptiness, restlessness, and guilt. This is accomplished with acceptance of the remedy for sin (God's invitation to accept His Son), washing in the pool of Christ's Blood (prescription to cure sin's effects), and being filled with the Inner Immanuel (the after-effect of being under His Control).

The great news concerning the side effects of the Holy Spirit is that they are not negative in their results, but Christians experience positive influences that bring fruit that is sweet to the taste buds of life. Paul wrote:

> But what happens when we live God's way? He brings gifts into our lives, much the same way that fruit appears in an orchard—things like affection for others, exuberance about life, serenity. We develop a willingness to stick with things, a sense of compassion in the heart, and a conviction that a basic holiness permeates things and people. We find ourselves involved in loyal commitments, not needing to force our way in life, able to marshal and direct our energies wisely. Legalism is helpless in bringing this about; it only gets in the way.
> (Galatians 5:22-23)

The fruit that produces love, joy, and peace are personal to me because they are a part of the redemption story. These three deal directly with our selves. The fruit that produces long-suffering, gentleness, and goodness are those that correspond with how we treat others. These three deal directly with our neighbors. The fruit that produces faith, meekness, and temperance determines our attitude, which reveals our ultimate growth in God. These three deal directly with our special relationship with God. The side effects of the Inner Immanuel and the fruit that is produced goes deeper into the life of a Christian by causing spiritual Selahs, spiritual stops to witness the holiness of God. Spiritual Selahs are the pauses, the meditations, which go on and on, and the beholding of the actions of God, Christ, and the Holy Spirit. They are the episodes in the walk of a Christian that make them stop and take notice to the moving of the Trinity in the universe, realizing that no one can do the things they can do. It makes the Christian a worshipper of the Most High during any and every situation in life. The English theologian Archbishop William Temple defines worship:

> Worship is to quicken the conscientious by the holiness of God to feed the mind by the truth of God, to purge to the love of God and to devote the will to the purpose of God.[4]

The Holy Spirit aids the Christian in being a worshipper and possessing the elements of worship of God. *Adoration*—spirit of reverence and respect; *Confession*—humility and repentance; *Forgiveness*—restores the worshippers; and *Dedication and commitment*—turns fellowship into ministry. It is in worshipping God that His Holiness causes Spiritual Selahs. Consider the holiness of God that caused Adam and Eve to hide from God in the garden. The holiness of God caused Moses to pause and take notice as in Genesis 4. He threw down his rod and it turned into a snake, and picking it up it turned back into a rod; putting his hand in his shirt and he came out with leprosy, and then put it back and it come out clean; or when he picked up some sand and by the time it hit the ground it turned to blood. The holiness of God caused Job's accusations to turn to adoration for God and by seeing God made him repent. The holiness of God caused John to fall down as a dead man. The holiness of God caused Peter, after the third time he denied the Christ, to go out and weep bitterly and cry out, "I am a sinful man." Saul saw God and declared, "My righteousness is garbage next to the holiness of God."

From time to time Spiritual Selahs come at the appointment of Heaven that then move to you and me to answering the call of Heaven to change the spiritual status quo. The Archbishop Desmond Tutu once said in the foreword of the book *A Dangerous Dozen* concerning "The Wind of God" that brings changes that are gone with the wind of heaven:

> Times change and situations seem to change, but there is still a great need for prophets, for God's ambassadors, to stand up and be counted. Who will dare to be Paul the Apostle today, or Dorothy Day, or Francis of Assisi, or Dietrich Bonhoeffer? Who will dare, when God calls, to say, "Here I am, Lord. Send me?"[5]

It is not enough to affect the status quo (the way things are now) by building a program of peace and prosperity. God turned a scribe into a prophet (Isaiah), who realized even though they were prospering physically, they were spiritually bankrupt. It's not OK to have fame and wealth while people are dying in the streets right before one's eyes and not be moved to lend a helping hand. When the day is dark who will assist others on the edge of being permanent residents that reside below the snake line? Who will point them to raising their heads to the hills, looking beyond the mountains for help, attitude adjustments, and revitalized confidence? Who will assist the spiritually bankrupt to see the Greatness of God, the Saving Hand of Christ, and the Empowering Presence of the Holy Spirit? Is there another like "Isabella" who experiences the Breath of God to change the status quo? In his book *A Dangerous Dozen*, C. K. Robertson writes of "Isabella":

> She later spoke of this spiritual awakening as "God's breath" that had come and filled her and made her a new person. For the next several years, she grew in her spiritual awareness as well as in her giftedness as a preacher.... She changed her name to Sojourner Truth. "The Spirit calls me, and I must go."[6]

Sojourner Truth, a positive "God-Talker," was an African American abolitionist and women's rights activist who heard the call of the Spirit to make a difference in the world. She was born into slavery in New York but escaped with her infant daughter to freedom in 1826. After going to court to recover her son, she became the first Black woman to win such a case against a white man.

Sojourner Truth was named Isabella Baumfree when she was born. She gave herself the name Sojourner Truth in 1843. Her best-known extemporaneous speech on gender inequalities, "Ain't I a Woman?" was delivered in 1851 at the Ohio Women's Rights Convention in Akron, Ohio. During the Civil War, Truth helped recruit Black troops for the Union Army; after the war, she tried unsuccessfully to secure land grants from the federal government for former slaves. This liberator of people with the Inner Immanuel changed the status quo by not settling for the way things are now but looking for the Hand of God to change the spiritually bankrupt, to having deposits made in the spirit realm. The side effects of the Holy Spirit will make the Christian move in a spiritually bankrupt world to have persons make spiritual deposits into the bank of Heaven. To experience Heaven's best will lead in walking a line that brings others in tow, to allow the Holy Spirit to produce the fruit that others can taste and later testify, "Oh taste and see that the Lord is good."

How many persons did Sojourner bring with her in tow? Better yet, how many persons have Christians across the universe brought in tow? These questions are better answered while walking the tightrope wire with the intention of not walking alone. The quest always must be the same. Who can the Christian with the aid of the Breath of God bring with us as we walk through this devalued world? The Spirit is still calling, asking, Will the Christian continue to go dropping rose petals of love from the Christ in the paths others walk? The Spirit is calling for more liberators like Isabella to change their names to God's lifeguards who free others from the 25-pound bricks that weigh them down and drown them in the sea of life.

WANTED: lifeguards who are "God-Talkers" to walk on water and reach down and pull drowning souls to the bank of God. It is true every lost soul has a "God-Talker" who answered the call of the Holy Spirit, but every Christian ought to be a "God-Talker" to someone. I was so tired of hearing the status quo of the state of the thugs of this world. Hearing the call of The Spirit, feeling if I could aid just one thug to turn into a positive "God-Talker," my life would not be in vain. The Spirit led this child of God to one of his students, thug to the 10th power. The Spirit arranged a meeting between us. The lifeguard of lives in the physical changed into being a lifeguard in the spiritual realm, and he is now preaching the Gospel. The side effects of the Holy Spirit can aid more lifeguards to change the status quo from what it is now to what it can become. Change agents, spiritual lifeguards are not afraid to get wet and are answering the call of the Holy Spirit in the midst of life's present challenges.

THE SPIRITUAL KINTSUKURIO PROCESS OF BEING EMPOWERED BY THE SPIRIT
"Lord, remake us"

Her story is heartbreaking to say the least. Many have had to fight this fight brought to the attention of those of us who regularly tune in to the *Tom Joyner Morning Show*. Her fight was an internal one—one that she lost when she took her own life. The news anchor reported on a battle that is waged against all of us at one time or another. It is a fight that must be waged between the hurts and pains of this life (sorrows) and experiencing the hopeful alternative of a bliss-filled world (joys). There is no doubt about it: all will have to struggle with brokenness, shattered hearts, natural and spiritual struggles, insecurities, low self-esteem, powerlessness, desperation, alienation, loneliness, and other major setbacks that leave persons broken into billions of pieces (the troubles of the world). The fight to get through these real-life episodes will come and the battle must be waged to win the fight. The young lady's story is not unique, for others have fought the same battle and lost the fight. They too gave up on life—taking the road too often traveled that ended their lives by committing suicide. Whatever their reason for carrying out this deed, the common thread that runs through this unfortunate event in each of the lives lost is that they gave up on life. Instead of fighting against the demonic spirits that can find entry into some weakened portal of the psyche, offering the end of life as the best way to end the unbearable pain that is being felt, many succumb to the seemingly easy way out, and surrender to death.

Unfortunately, in the heat of the battle, rarely does the target of these demonic attacks seek professional aid to fight the fight for remaking, reassessing, and reframing great personal tragedies into a life with great testimonies of triumph. I wish I could have been there to share with those who have thrown in the towel on life a personal testament that "He can bring you through the darkest of nights and the coldest of days." The Inner Immanuel is waiting and willing to give relief from struggle. However, He will not make anyone accept His presence, power, and dynamic movement. It is an invitation that has to be received which requires submission and yielding to His Authority. He will not force Himself upon anyone but will make known that He is available and ready to make the difference by His multi-dimensional power—His Comforting power, His Guiding power, and His Healing power.

Many persons have lived through difficult times, are going through difficult times, or are on their way into difficult times. Yet any of these can be overcome by leaning on a genuine belief and faith in the Third Person of the Trinity—the Holy Ghost! Since time began, He has carried persons through adverse circumstances, insurmountable odds, and hostile environments, no matter how unpleasant, and healed their brokenness by penetrating every nook and cranny of their world with His Power. It is the healing balm for their damaged world, filling them with the glue of grace and that becomes their change agent of deific hope (heavenly hope). From one moment to the next, around any corner, the flow of His existence can happen to any person, in any class of "God-Talkers," and they can be faced with experiencing life as did "Humpty Dumpty" in the nursery rhyme and find themselves falling off the wall of life. They, too, could be broken into billions of pieces and feel that there is no aid to put them back together again. From a physical viewpoint, there would be no amount of money, influence, or know-how able to put brokenness in mind, heart, and soul back together from the daunting dilemmas that are often part of living as human beings. If only it were possible to skip over the pain, hurt, and helplessness of life, the bouts of crying, depression, and hopelessness. However, life is really about looking at the scary part of life squarely in the eye, accessing and making sense of where you've been, what you've lived through, and embracing one's weaknesses as finite beings.

This "God-Talker" would have liked to listen to the news show explore how a professional could reframe hurt and hear the difference that can come from talking with a trained Christian counselor who specializes in dealing with putting broken pieces back together. Mental health is crucial to facing life bravely, constructively, and fighting with resilience second by second, hour by hour, and day by day; to keep putting one foot in front of the other until the pieces begin to come back into place.

I have been there, in the place of no pastures. I wrote concerning the unending fight to be more beautiful after the brokenness because beauty does come from brokenness. I write in our fifth book, *Surviving Category 5 Heartaches,* of the fight for my mental health in the face of wanting to leave this world because the pain was too much to bear and seemed too great to overcome:

> I would be alone with my thoughts. As soon as my children hugged and kissed me goodbye and walked out of my apartment door, I immediately went to lie down and burst into tears. I recall balling up into a fetal position and crying nonstop for more than three hours. The devil began to speak to my mind, saying, "You have some razors...just cut your wrist and it will all be over." I listened to his words and decided to take his advice. I reached into my kitchen cabinet and pulled out the Jack Daniels bottle that I had hidden there for medicinal purposes. I retrieved the razors from the bathroom cabinet and started running water in the tub. I recall drinking several shots of whiskey, taking off my clothes and getting into the water. By this time, my right vein began to speak to me, "Cut me and lay back into the water... it will all be over

soon." As I reached for the razors, however, God intervened, saying, "If you do this, who will preach at your student's church this Sunday? You know you are scheduled to preach." At that second I replied to God, "You are right. I am on to preach and I must get ready." I took a bath, returned the Jack Daniels back into the kitchen cabinet and the razors back into the bathroom cabinet and reached for my little black Bible.[7]

I had the Inner Immanuel speaking to me and telling me to stop listening to the voice of the devil. As I listened to the radio that day, inside of my being I cried for this young lady who seemingly had no "little black Bible to reach for." So, she took her life after the death of her mother and other struggles. To feel overwhelming grief, weeping day and night, being down-hearted, having bitterness of the soul, in constant misery, deeply troubled, and grappling with great amounts of anguish can lead one to want to end his/her journey on this planet. It's sad to say but very true that at some point in time every "God-Talker" will have to decide whether to listen to the Inner Immanuel or fall off the wall and onto the ground shattering into billions of pieces with no hope of ever being put back together again.

Let us first acknowledge that these feelings are very real and have to be dealt with constructively. Reaching for the Great Comforter of life is the best option. Unfortunately, so many attempt to deal with the pain of life by drinking their way out, sniffing their way out, smoking their way out, or sleeping their way out, and without ever realizing that the Inner Immanuel is their only way out of the misery and suffering that all must face in this life. The battle is fought in victory with Him working inside of one's mind, heart, and soul, providing the inner strength and the anchor to hold you and me until our change comes and the pain begins to subside.

One day while reading Facebook I was introduced to the story of Kintsugi, or Kintsukuroi. This story gives much credence to looking at the struggles of this life from a different perspective. This different perspective inspires all of God's children to realize they are going to have to deal with the struggles of this life. But how one manages their struggles is the key. From the biblical perspective Hannah dealt with her struggles by continuing to seek the face of God, Elijah dealt with his struggles by waiting on God to continue to show strong on his behalf, and Paul dealt with his struggles by receiving something he never had before in his life until the Christ spoke "Amazing Grace" to him on the Damascus Road.

Consider looking at your struggles through this Japanese word Kintsukuroi. It is pronounced, according to the Google translator, *kint-ska-roy-e*. The contextual reference for this word and its meaning for us today began with a story dating back to the late 15th century, when a Japanese Shogun sent a damaged Chinese tea bowl back to China to be fixed. It was returned held together with ugly metal staples, launching the Japanese craftsmen on a quest for a new form of repair that could make a broken piece look as good as new, or better. Kintsukuroi means to "repair with gold." Kintsukuroi is the tradition of repairing broken pottery with gold or silver. By using this method, they express an understanding that the piece is more beautiful for having been broken. I invite you to Google Kintsukuroi for further discovery of the beauty of this great art.

Take a look at still another beautiful example the Japanese masters have given to the world through this great Kintsukuroi process and technique of fixing what has been broken and making it become better than it was before the breaking. It is a difficult and intensive process requiring no small amount of skill, but when the broken item is fixed, it is adorned with veins of precious metal and is thus made even more beautiful than it was originally. The craftsmen use the technique of lacquer, a clear or colored wood finish that dries by solvent evaporation or a curing process that produces a hard, durable finish. "What a spiritually moving thought that is," I said to myself. To receive spiritual therapy from the Inner Immanuel that will cause not just natural Kintsukuroi but spiritual Kintsukuroi. Spiritual Kintsukuroi would be the Christian's repair from being broken and upon being put back together again made better than before the break. Wow! It gives new meaning to the phrase "being better and not bitter," "looking different than what I have been through," and "if you only knew the trouble I have seen."

Now it doesn't seem to go too far if we say, "I have been through the process of spiritual Kint-ska-roy-e." We can see its scriptural kinship to the process of God using Heavenly gold upon the "God-Talkers" who have been up the rough side of the mountain and have fallen down, breaking things in the natural and spiritual realm, and God repairing them on His potter's wheel. Imagine the gold of God running through our brokenness and as our hearts beat pumping blood through our veins, God pumps the gold of Heaven, the silver of Heaven through our natural and spiritual bodies, attacking, fixing, repairing, refurbishing, and restoring everything that is hurting you and me. He leaves spiritual veins as a testament of His Glory and healing power. As the Inner Immanuel who skillfully and masterfully places Heaven's gold and silver in our wounds it becomes the balm to heal and hold His children together through the rough seasons of our lives. Mothers will die, wives and husbands may leave, fathers will not claim their children or raise their children, but spiritual Kintsukuroi will be present to give a new testimony from devastating and disheartening episodes in life, declaring the Inner Immanuel has brought joy into my world for all the sorrow that has been experienced. "God-Talkers" may then testify to the gold (being His grace) and the silver (being His mercy) that held and continually holds you and me together as piece by piece is put securely, comfortingly, and lovingly back in place, making the "God-Talker" better than before the brokenness. God places spiritual lacquer over the Christian theist, covering the "God-Talker" with a strong finish over the wounds to make sure they heal completely and provides a Heavenly finish for all to see that our God brought us through!

Life can shatter the strongest among us and cracks can still come when an event close to one's mind, heart, and soul brings one to their knees screaming,

"Nothing hurts but I feel pain all over." The Inner Immanuel specializes in such pain and aids in the fight against suicidal thoughts, depression, alienation, isolation, shame, loneliness, and abandonment. The fight must be fought to regain normalcy in one's world and move from allowing negative thoughts and experiences to cut one off from the light. The light can be gained from moving to the positive side of life that boasts and can testify that "there is a crack in everything and that's really how the light gets into our worlds." The key is remembering to reach for the spiritual Kint-ska-roy-e to start the process on the road to recovery, to healing and wholeness, and to allow spiritual lacquering to cover us with Heavenly dew.

The process of spiritual Kintsukuroi begins by letting earth and Heaven be a part of using gold (grace) and silver (mercy) in the places of pain and hurt. Then yield to spiritual lacquering refreshing presence to be the finish that shines from the inside out. The process has to begin with acknowledging the need to be worked on by professional caregivers, trained Christian counselors, and allowing the Inner Immanuel to work on the broken clay through them as conduits of His healing and wholeness potter's wheel. Consequently, the process for being empowered to overcome the hurts and pains of this world is to stand on these eight helpful thoughts as the best way to triumph over the many sorrows that are thrown our way and to see the situation in a different light, never forgetting that the pain is very real but the remedy is very powerful. These eight thoughts give a positive spin to negative situations:

- First, keep this spiritual truth in the forefront of your mind, heart, and soul. There will be no pause in my Praise to God. No matter how great the pain, struggle, and hurts, never let there be a lapse or interruption in Giving God the Praise He should be given. If you pause, spiritual Kintsukuroi cannot have its full benefit to the Christian. It can prevent your heart from mending. Reference Scriptures: Matthew 6:33; 1 Corinthians 1:31; Philippians 4:19.

- Secondly, let the Holy Spirit stop the Christian from making the crucial mistake of living in the dark shadows and shame of pain. While you're in the storm, the safest place to be is in His Hands and not in the tears you have cried. Missing church and electing to stay home to have church with your scars, depression, and disconnection to the throne is not recommended. If one has to fall off into church crawling on hands and knees, go to the House of God! This is the time when you need to hear and hold on to every Scripture passage you have ever read, loved, and written in your heart. The House of God is where your will receive strength to keep pushing in the mist of pain. Reference Scriptures: Ephesians 6:10; Nehemiah 6:9; Psalm 27:13.
- Thirdly, the "God-Talker" has to fight to be resurrected from the brink of the Abyss. Moving from the black hole will be the hardest fight one has ever fought. Fighting back after reaching emotional rock bottom can be done but you can never stop the process of being reshaped, reformed, and reestablished into Heavenly places. Never forget that the Inner Immanuel will aid and comfort. Wiping away your tears, holding you, and rocking you to sleep is His job and He loves to show He cares. And health professionals stand in wait to be used to assist with helping you achieve emotional stability. Reference Scriptures: Psalm 20:4; Proverbs 12:15; Revelation 3:18.
- Fourthly, the Holy Spirit has been performing spiritual Kintsukuroi since He showed up in this world. He has been aiding "God-Talkers" who have put into practice a progressive knowledge of God and belief in the Christ to overcome desert, famine, and barren and drought seasons. He continues to bring in renewed vigor to continue to fight against the enemies of one's mind, heart, and soul. He gives the power required to weather the storms of life bravely because of Him being our Comforter. Reference Scriptures: Psalm 23:4; 119:50; Matthew 9:22.

- Fifthly, to reign with Christ one has to suffer for the cause of Heaven. The Christian theist is not exempt from the hardships that come along with being a living and breathing creature made in His image. Suffering knows every Christian's address. Job teaches this truth that Satan is looking to get permission to try your resolve and commitment to the Kingdom. Permission has to be given before Satan can make his attack. If God allows him to come be assured He will give what is needed to win the fight. You are more than a conqueror no matter what. Reference Scriptures: Philippians 3:10; James 5:10; Psalm 55:22.
- Sixthly, before the Christian goes into the nighttime get your lamps filled with oil and get some to put in reserve. No one prepares for testing in the test. It's always before the test. Nighttime is coming to every human being. But to be prepared for the dark get ready in the light and fill up at the spiritual fuel station every day. Prayer, fasting, worship, praise, and studying the Word of the Bible gets you ready for what is to surely come—Tests, Trials, and Tribulations. Wandering aimlessly around in the dark of night one finds it difficult to navigate through empty pleasures, positions, and pursuits with nothing to anchor one's soul. Dark seasons of pain require the Holy Spirit to heal and carry us throughout our lives. Reference Scriptures: Matthew 4:4; John 6:35; 14:6.
- Seventhly, Spiritual Kintsukuroi is a testimony of the Christian declaring that what has been gone through has made them better than they could have ever imagined in concrete ways. Stronger belief and faith, side effects of the Holy Spirit, fuel the "God-Talker" to continue having spiritual Selahs, to sin less, and to become spiritual lifeguards. We are brought to the conclusion that spiritual struggles take the child of God to another level and the empowering force of the Inner Immanuel is the difference. Reference Scriptures: Genesis 32:24; 2 Corinthians 4:9; Romans 8:28.

- Lastly, time after time He, the Comforter, the Guide, and the Teacher, makes His presence felt, especially in times of heartache, pain, and suffering. He walks alongside of "God-Talkers," propping the Christian up on every side; speaking gentle words that fortify our well-being, security, and contentment. The Holy Spirit is in us, moving through us, and alongside of us desiring to make His mark on the life of the broken, battered, and bruised by giving hope where there is despair. Reference Scriptures: Zechariah 4:6; Ephesians 5:18; 1 Thessalonians 4:8.

Reframing the hurt and pain is the key to these eight thoughts being the powerful moving force of positive thinking to aid in bringing the light of healing and wholeness into dark worlds. Make no mistake about it: there will be tragedy, but it can be and must be made over with the power of the Holy Spirit. Amen.

THE SPIRITUAL KAIZEN EXPERIENCE OF BEING EMPOWERED BY THE SPIRIT

"Afraid of change no longer"

Humankind is restless, sometimes hopeless, wandering and defeated, needing a spark from the inside of their being to turn negative experiences into positive ones. We are always in search of the answer—turning over every rock and looking into every possibility to change an unbalanced walk. Lost in the wilderness of this world, humankind needs relief from the tireless journey of perpetual pursuit of contentment, gratification, and serenity. The Maker of all that exists waits for the second, the moment, and the hour that one of us will experience spiritual turbulence to offset any unbalanced walk. The fathers of the faith, Abraham, Isaac, and Jacob, were in need of this spiritual turbulence. The mothers of the faith, Rahab, Rizpah, and Naomi, sought this spiritual turbulence. The prophets Jeremiah, Isaiah, and Ezekiel thirsted for such spiritual turbulence. If this disturbs you, Eureka! I have your attention. It affords me the opportunity to offer you a different perspective on something that would ordinarily be associated with chaos, confusion, and turmoil. However, let's look at it from the spiritual realm. The Spiritual turbulence of which we speak is the movement of the Holy Spirit that disrupts in a positive manner and brings life-altering transformation to a person's world, making their lives richer in joy, peace, and wholeness. Spiritual turbulence is marked by radical change that is for the betterment of the person who is at a turning point in their walk with God.

In Margaret Mitchell's book *Gone with the Wind*, the author chronicles the changes that occurred throughout the South during the Civil War that altered people's lives for the better. Change, positive change, marked their turning point. This is what the Christ did for His disciples of old and His new disciples today in John 20:20-21:

> The disciples, seeing the Master with their own eyes, were exuberant. Jesus repeated his greeting: "Peace to you. Just as the Father sent me, I send you." Then he took a deep breath and breathed into them. "Receive the Holy Spirit," he said.

Christ changed their lives and the Christian's life for the better because at the crossroad of change, the breathing of the Holy Spirit marked a major change that was on the way. Christ breathed into their inner tabernacles, and they received the Power to do the will of God. This special filling would usher in a new age for Christians across the annals of time. It ushered in a radical change for those who would no longer seek to do God's work on their own. They would be filled with the guidance He provides to do His Will, both His general and specific will. They would adhere to His general will, which is to tell others of His Saving Power from an unbalanced walk of life. They would be able to stand tall and take the hits and blows from a mean and cruel world as this New Shekinah glory moved from the outer temple to the inner temple. This was a radical change in thought for the people of that day to experience God not just in a place or building as a temple of God but in a different temple, an inner temple where the Inner Immanuel would now take up residence. This new thought would introduce believers to a new dimension of God, causing super-natural power to move from the place of God (the tabernacle) into the people of God (inner tabernacles), providing a Holy presence that would cause the Christian theist to brave life as the Power of the breath of Heaven supernaturally fills them to become "God-Talkers." This change came to make us better and stronger as a result of His wounded hands and side testifying "The Inner Immanuel has been breathed into your spiritual lungs."

The specific will of God needs this new Shekinah Glory to use God-given talents and God-given gifts to create an army of disciples that will carry out the Christian's specific tasks of aiding in changing the Status Quo.

In this day and time "God-Talkers" have received this spiritual turbulence not just in a tabernacle, tent, or church but on the inside of their triune beings. Yes, the Inner Immanuel has transformed the natural bodies of Christians into the dwelling and settling place where God can reside and God can get the glory. The Divine Presence of God is not just in the tabernacle, tent, or church. He has taken up residence in a new temple. The new Shekinah Glory has tabernacle inside humankind to make the unbalanced walk balanced. This Power moves in and evicts restlessness, hopelessness, rootlessness, and the agony of defeat. It allows the invisible God to become visible in the presence of a Friendly Holy Ghost. The New Shekinah is the spiritual turbulence that starts from the inside and works His way to the outside with the hope that spiritual turbulence and transformation will come in five areas of radical change for the better by:

- Transforming "God-Talkers" into being Heaven's "fairest." He sees in Christians the light, life, and love of Christ and Holy Spirit to work in, on, and through us.
- Transforming "God-Talkers" to go "forth." He guides Christians to reach out to others in the world, encouraging them to receive the Holy Spirit.

- Transforming "God-Talkers" to take "footsteps." He pushes the Christian to walk in paths that are ordered by Him.
- Transforming "God-Talkers" to stand as one "flock." He hopes that the Christian will come together and do His general will and specific will in the world.
- Transforming "God-Talkers" to "feed." He trusts that the Christian will care for those believers who are younger than we are so that they may grow into mature Christians.

Spiritual turbulence and transformation are essential for these five thoughts to become reality. If they are not present, the choir can be singing, prayers are being uttered, and the word is being preached, yet something is missing. Is it the passion of the worshippers? Is it the celebration of the delivered? Or is it the delighted confessions? The edifice is immaculate, the landscape is beautiful, and the furnishings are pristine, yet something is wrong. Is there a crack in the foundation? Is there a leaky roof? Is it a structural problem? The church bells ring throughout the distance, the steeple lights up in the darkness, and the marquee flashes with upcoming events, yet something is lacking. Is it the reputation of the fellowship? Is it the relationship or lack of relationship with the community? Or is it the leaders of the church? NO! What is missing, what is lacking, what is wrong is that God is not there because the Inner Immanuel has not moved from the outer tabernacle into the inner tabernacle! What must take place for the positive "God-Talker" is a shifting in the atmosphere from outer to inner.

The second Japanese word I'd like to mention for the Christian encouragement is *Kaizen*. This word is pronounced *kie-zen*, and it means change but not just any kind of change. It's change that leads toward constant improvement, constant development, and continuous change for the better. It's a good change, a great change, a mos-needed change, and a radical change. Speaking spiritual Kaizen would be a Godly change brought on by the Inner Immanuel that causes constant improvement through growth in knowledge, belief, and empowerment to do God's general and specific will in this world. Constant development of the Christian requires growing in grace to the extent of being a change agent in this life. Continuous change is a must for the "God-Talker" to find more ways to exercise the *Insanity of Theology* in their own lives and aid in the lives of others. The new Shekinah moves beyond the outer tabernacle into the inner tabernacle, producing change agents who seek to aid in the change of the inner tabernacles of others; change that is constantly and continually performing the general and specific will of God in this world.

God has given "God-Talkers" jobs and job descriptions to perform in this world. The call to serve this present age has to be answered. Notice that the job of "God-Talkers" is to receive the Inner Immanuel to the extent that the new Shekinah transforms the triune parts to affect the outer parts of the "God-Talker" and of humankind as I see it:

The Inner Immanuel as Spiritual Kaizen

He changes our eyes—our natural eyes to spiritual eyes that tell of spiritual depth. Behind the veil of these eyes are the blemishes of sin that have been replaced with the blessedness of being empowered. His transforming work has replaced our ashes with beauty, mourning with the oil of joy, and heaviness with the garment of praise.

He changes our hair—representing our understanding of the code that must be kept. It is the same code broken by Samson in Judges 16:20 —the code of concentration and gratefulness for strength from Him and the unwavering support provided by the Trinity. It acknowledges that "God-Talkers" are aware of His presence, power, and the dynamic movement of His spirit; and knowing these things, Christian theists desire to be obedient to Him.

He changes our teeth—teeth that are white and shining because we have grown up in wisdom and stature. We now have the ability to receive the good news, understand the good news, and apply the good news in our everyday living while exercising the "*Insanity of Theology*."

He changes our lips—they are the new creation that speak life instead of death, blessing instead of cursing, and joy instead of strife.

Christians now testify of our new life in Christ, for "God-Talkers" have clean lips that have been sanctified in His blood.

He changes our temples and cheeks—they are indicative of the genuine expressions that come from the inside out. The New Shekinah is changing us from the inside out from being humankind to being God-kind. No longer hidden, the overflowing change shows forth, outwardly. The joy of the Lord shows through discouragement, sorrow, and heartache. Outside forces can no longer affect "God-Talkers'" outward appearance, for our expressions are birthed from changed triune beings.

He changes our necks—gone is the stiffness, stubbornness, and selfishness of the old life, transformed into a pliable mind and malleable heart that infuses the Christian's soul and characterizes the concept of true beauty that can only come from the Inner Immanuel. He has replaced our self-will and produced spiritual Kaizen, constant improvement, constant and continuous change.

He changes our breasts—our separation from the world and the bondage of Satan. The Christian's belief and faith produces an atmosphere and environment for feeding and growing. No longer is the Christian seeking the pleasures of the world but desiring that spiritual Kaizen be exercised every day as good change is the order of the day.

Spiritual turbulence, transformation, and radical change for the Christian moves from the outer tabernacle into the inner tabernacle as these seven moving points depict. This radical change is the direct result of receiving the Presence, Power, and Dynamic movement of the Inner Immanuel to directly and positively affect the changing of unbalanced living to balanced living. This causes a realization that the evidence of balanced living is allowing the breathing of the Holy Spirit to change the Christian into changing the location of the indwelling. When the change, radical change, took hold of the disciples, and especially Peter, Peter's balance was marked by being more consistent in his testimony, having constant improvement in his witness and continuous change in doing the general and specific will of God.

God-Talker's Mantra
"Keep the Flame burning bright"

The Love of My Life, Muriel, and I went shopping for household items. We purchased toiletries, skin care products, and scented candles that came with a top covering. I paid close attention to the scented candles because of my fondness for having them lit while meditating in the bathtub. When the meditating and bath are completed, I usually take the top of the candle and cover the flame. The burning flame usually takes several seconds to go out as the flame has no oxygen to fuel the fire. Recently, I went through my routine of lighting the scented candle and meditating in the bathtub and then covering the burning flame. But on this occasion, the Inner Immanuel spoke to me concerning how God-Talkers allow something or someone to cover the Flame of the Holy Spirit and put out His Flame. Allowing the covering of something or someone will deprive the Holy Spirit of being the spiritual oxygen needed to influence all who seek His presence.

Since one of the emblems of the Holy Spirit is Fire (the others are Water, Rain, Rivers, The Dew, The Wind, The Oil, The Dove, The Holy Anointing Oil, and The Seal), the burning candle to me represents "The Fire" of God. The Fire of God fuels the spiritual oxygen that gives life and brings three important thoughts to consider in keeping one's flame burning. The Fire (flame) brings God's presence, God's passion, and God's purity into the environment and into every circumstance. There are three things a Child of God cannot afford to go without while performing God's general will (telling others about Christ) and God's specific will (using God-given talents and God-given gifts to build up the Kingdom). The unending challenge for the servant of God is to keep the fire burning at all costs and flee the area of anything or anyone who intends to cut off the flow of the spiritual oxygen. The Christian needs the presence of God to lead, guide, and comfort. The Christian also requires the passion of God to fuel our ministry pursuits until their completion. Most importantly, the Christian must have the purity of God to clean up one's motives, virtues, and integrity.

The constant fight is one of not allowing sin, relationships, jobs, or personal pursuits to cover the flame of God's Spirit in the "God-Talkers'" lives. The only way this is to be achieved is to always "Dare Greatly" when it comes to allowing the Inner Immanuel to have the authority to fill Christians every second, every minute, and every hour of the day. The Christian is continually yielding to the Holy Spirit so that His presence, power, and dynamic movement are manifest as we constantly seek improvement in living out the Holy Bible. This requires our earnestly asking for the movement of the Holy Ghost to provide constant and continuous change in the Christian's behavior, actions, and motives with regard to the general and specific will of God. It was Teddy Roosevelt who stated:

> It is not the critic who counts: not the man who points out how the strong man stumbles or where the doer of deeds could have done better. The credit belongs to the man who is actually in the arena, whose face is marred by dust and sweat and blood, who strives valiantly, who errs and comes up short again and again; because there is no effort without error or shortcoming, but who knows the great enthusiasms, the great devotions, who spends himself for a worthy cause; who, at the best, knows, in the end, the triumph of high achievement, and who, at the worst, if he fails, at least he fails while daring greatly, so that his place shall never be with those cold and timid souls who knew neither victory nor defeat.[8]

Anyone can say he/she is trying, making an effort, or giving it his or her best shot. But to "Dare Greatly" requires more than trying, making an effort, or a best shot. It requires "God-Talkers" who will submit to the constant fight, under the authority of the Holy Spirit's "Fire" to burn within—infused with the supplying spiritual oxygen that brings certain victory. God's presence, passion, and purity have to be "Dared Greatly" to obtain God's desired end. What is God's desired end? For you and me to be more like The Christ.

In the Gospel of John, the army of the King is growing into special groups of believers. This group that assembles is becoming the product of spending quality time with the Trinity. Witness these people transform into His Image and take on the Mission of the Trinity everywhere they go. Starting out as dirt that has been touched by the God of Heaven, they are turned into His likeness. The Trinity kisses us on our lips and we kiss them back. See them crawling, walking, jogging, and running toward the Jordan river. See them march one by one, two by two, and three by three. They are following Christ into the River Jordan to go down in their sinful graves and rise up into new creatures breathed upon by His Wind. They cross into a new land, the promised land, the sacred land, the natural and spiritual land of companionship that is shared with the Second Adam. Onlookers can see them marching from the east, stepping to the west, and from the south, stepping to the north, singing. What song, do you ask? Singing the song "Steal away, Steal away, down by the Riverside."

Chapter 4

The Church That Gathers Down by the Riverside

THE INNER VESTMENT OF THE AUTHENTIC CHURCH

"The pursuit of the House of Heaven is to be clothed in Blood-washed garments"

God came near and nearer to His Creation, wanting, seeking, and asking His Creation to accept the promise, the promise He would be for His Creation. The covenant that was made could not be severed and it would be eternal. He pitched His tent on the edge of the heavens and at the fingertips of humankind in the Person of The Christ. Pledging His Divine Love as heavenly and earthly witnesses watched the walk that made Heaven and earth hush in silence, He gave up His life, His Blood, and Died for a devalued world on the cross. His tractor beam, The Inner Immanuel, drew the triune parts of His Creation to Him, offering His living soul's redemption from the sins of the first Adam. The Trinity came together to give the world the most fulfilling, satisfying, gratifying, and nourishing gift that could ever be given from a Creator to His creation—The Ultimate Kiss! It was the divine kiss of love, affection, ownership, protection, and transformation, a royal kiss that leads to a royal marriage between The Trinity and the triune parts of humankind. It is the Ultimate Kiss of Christ's Atonement from the cross and Blood of Immanuel. Atonement (the doctrine that describes how human beings can be reconciled to God) is how the Ultimate Kiss came into a devalued world. Christ's Atonement (the forgiving or pardoning of sin through the death, blood, and resurrection of Jesus Christ) restored harmony between humankind and the Throne of God and that is how abundant life can be achieved. It is this Ultimate Kiss that would produce and create the most powerful organism in the universe, The Authentic Church!

By definition the Authentic Church comprises those persons who have been called out of the world to go back into the same world telling others of His works and words in the natural and spiritual realms. The Ultimate Kiss brings divinity to death and produces abundant life. The Authentic Church is the "called-out ones." It is a part of a growing active communion of likeminded persons who seek to be a part of God's Kingdom. The Authentic Church is characterized by the five (5) things an Authentic Church does on the inside of the building or campus or tabernacle:

- **Worship**—Worshippers who have reasons to allow the inner reality of being influenced, inspired, and instructed by The Trinity to show up on the outside of one's life in natural and spiritual ways.
- **Fellowship**—The caring and sharing atmosphere that Christians feel when surrounded by other likeminded persons communing under the spiritual banner of the Christ. Individuals who reach up to God and out to humankind. "God-Talkers" who care and share with one another.
- **Teaching**—Using the Holy Bible and the Truth it dispenses to declare what is good and acceptable to the Godhead and living for the cause of Christ.
- **Preaching**—Preaching the Gospel of Christ. He lived, died, was buried and rose from the dead. Telling the story to the poor, the brokenhearted,

and those bound by the chains of the demonic. The acceptable year of deliverance is at hand.

- **Stewardship**—Using God-given talents and God-given gifts to further the causes of Heaven. Realizing that the Authentic Church is God's by ownership and the Christian theist by what we do for the general and specific will of God. It is the using of time, talent, treasure, influence, and opportunity to continue the carrying out of the Great Commission.

There are two things an Authentic Church does outside the church building or campus:

- **Christian Service**—that promotes healing and wholeness to persons outside of a Church building or campus or tabernacle. Encouraging persons who are lost in the sea of sin to accept the lifeline and gather with other sinners who have been saved by Grace.
- **Witnessing**—witnessing to the thoughts of Christ; what is seen and heard through the natural and spiritual actions of The Trinity. Having compassion along with a testimony that communicates the power of the Inner Immanuel and a Christian who has been saved by Heaven's Lifeguard. Telling the story that the "God-Talker" has been by Calvary, had his sins forgiven, and experiences Pentecost to receive the power that draws the Christian down by the Riverside.

These are the seven things an Authentic Church does when the Power of The Trinity is present. The Authentic Church is not a building or campus or tabernacle, although buildings or campuses or tabernacles are used. It is a Church Without Walls as its occupants leave the building and spread out into the world. It is a body of born-again believers who perform the general and specific will of the Almighty God. The Authentic Church turns a devalued world upside down, inside out, and right side up for the sole purpose of growing individuals and corporate bodies into the image of Christ. I see The Authentic Church defined as:

The Authentic Church body of believers has been brought into existence by the Flame and Fire of the Inner Immanuel, the flame that burns on the inside of the body and spreads as fire on the outside. It becomes a continual growing body of born-again believers who grow inside the building or campus or tabernacle, bursting forth from seams of overflowing worship and fellowship to the outside of the building and dropping rose petals of love and service as signs of The Trinity's love everywhere one goes. This becomes the result of the Flame and Fire of the Inner Immanuel creating a never-dying and never-ending move of God. What an awesome privilege it is to be a part of an ongoing enterprise, a caring and sharing organism in the business of saving lost souls and caring for others; to be one among the born-again body of believers who reach up to God and out to humankind.

The organism that is birthed from this Ultimate Kiss brings divinity to death and produces abundant life that is living, breathing, fresh, growing, moving, transforming, renewing, new verve power between God's Son Jesus and the "But as many as receive Him" crowd. This group would become the first assembly to be called the "Church," and later to be called "Christians." The word church is found 115 times in the New Testament and translated three times as "Assembly." Church is translated in the Greek text from the word *ekklesia,* which means:

> A company of Christians, or of those who, hoping for eternal salvation through Jesus Christ, observe their own religious rites, hold their own religious meetings, and manage their own affairs, according to regulations prescribed for the body for order's sake.[1]

The Ekklesia, the Church, is a union between Christ and His "But as many as receive Him" group and is a match made in the heavens. It is an organism that is brought to life by the Inner Immanuel. Yes, there have been great unions before such as the union of Christ being the Head and the "But as many as receive Him" group being the body; this can be called "the living union." There is also the Christ as the Foundation and the "But as many as receive Him" group as the building, "the lasting union." Not to mention the Christ as the Vine and the "But as many as receive Him" group being the branches, the "fruitful union." And still not forgetting the Christ as the Firstborn and the "But as many as receive

Him" group being His brethren, the "joint-heirs union." These are great unions between the Christ and the "But as many as receive Him" group. Yet the most important, most beneficial, most loving, most heartwarming, and most sacred is The Trinity's Kiss that produces the Christ as the Bridegroom and the "But as many as receive Him" group as His bride, The Church; this is the "loving union."

This loving union between the Christ and the "But as many as receive Him" group (the Authentic Church) is legendary and is always the prominent headline in the Heaven Chronicle Today Newspaper. Consider that there is an individual group of the "But as many as receive Him" assembly, and there is a corporate group of "But as many as receive Him." These are the two groups John declares as the organism of God that He "Gave them the power to become" and the power to overcome. We observe this walking through the Gospel of John:

- Peter, Nathaniel, etc. (John 1:35-51).
- The ruler Nicodemus (John 3:1-21).
- The Sychar woman (John 4:6-26).
- The man born blind (John 9: 35-41).
- Martha and Mary (John 11).
- The eleven apostles (John 13-16).
- Mary Magdalene (John 20:1-18).
- The apostle Peter (John 21:15-23).

These two groups—individuals and small groups—were the "But as many as receive Him" group that The Trinity gave the "Power to become" and the power to overcome as John 1:12 declares:

> But whoever did want him, who believed he was
> who he claimed and would do what he said, He made
> to be their true selves, their child-of-God selves.

What has The Trinity given to these two groups of persons? The Trinity has given them Their Ultimate Kisses. What could be better for these two groups of persons? The Trinity has given them Their Divine love. What is the power that can't be escaped? It is the power of Their love, presence, and natural and spiritual actions. The Trinity has given them the promise of more of Their Ultimate Kisses, demonstrating The Trinity's faithful allegiance. Since The Trinity is giving Ultimate Kisses, friendship and fellowship will replace loneliness and separation. Their affection and communion dispel coldness and betrayal and rekindle warmth and loyalty. Their Ultimate Kisses of substance and enjoyment restore fulfillment and joy where once there was emptiness and sadness. They transform. Thus, the dissatisfaction of conventional relationships with Provincial "God-Talkers" becomes a relentless individual pursuit of affection given to The Trinity. As the organism of God passes by, transformation happens to more people who desire to join the group of the individual and corporate "But as many as receive Him" crowd, and in their rush to receive the Kiss of Christ, cast their burdens of sadness, disease, paralysis, hunger, anxiety, darkness, death, frustration, and failure by the side of the riverbank. The organism picks up and gives the new persons who join The Church the power to feel and experience gladness, health, energy, fullness, peace, light and life, natural and spiritual success. Down by the riverside The Trinity's presence provides an overflow and the two groups experience natural and spiritual bliss! These two groups shout and testify that His Blood made the following a reality as I see it:

> The Trinity's Love is paid for—there is no cost.
>
> The Trinity's love will never grow sour; it only grows sweeter.
>
> The Trinity's Love is a thirst quencher. Trying all the other wines of the world is not necessary—they pale in comparison.
>
> The Trinity's Love has no ill effects, only benefits.
>
> The Trinity's Love is deposited with a kiss that is unconditional, freely given.
>
> The Trinity's Kiss soothes the mind, body, and soul.
>
> The Trinity's Love is the best love of the best.

The Trinity's love is so good it is almost insanely unimaginable! Yet, The Trinity's Love pursues us and then draws you and me into a deepening union with Them. The magnet of Their love pulls "God-Talkers" from the enemy's captivity. On our own, the pulling power of the world, the flesh, and the devil is overwhelming. However, with the aid of the Holy Spirit it can be conquered. Consequently, the outcry of the "But as many as receive Him" group must be in unison, asking that:

- "God-Talkers" be set free from the shackles of the oppressor and be drawn closer to God (John 6:44).
- "God-Talkers" have every crack and crevice yearning for the Christ to fill it with His drawing power (John 12:32).
- "God-Talkers" have each part of the "But as many as receive Him" group who seeks the Ultimate Kiss that assures victory from the quiet hells so prevalent in life (John 16:13-15).

It is the quest to possess the inner beauty and glory of The Trinity and to see into these three personalities that enraptures our being, overflows spiritual cups, and infuses gold and silver into our hurting inner places. God the Father, God the Son, and God the Holy Spirit insure these groups never have to face life below the snake line. The drawing power of God pulls "God-Talkers" individually and corporately away from the first Adam's curse and draws us to the saving power of the second Adam's cure. It beckons "Provincial," "Practical," "Pastoral," "Prophetic," and "Professional" God-Talkers away from the world's influences that would encourage them to run after the vanities of life, seeking everything except the Kingdom of God and His righteousness (Matt. 6:33). It calls "Prospective God-Talkers" away from the lust of the flesh, the lust of the eyes, and the lust of the heart, seeking to please me, me, and me. It calls the "But as many as receive Him" group away from the influence of the fallen angel who seeks to devour all who come in his path and skillfully deceives many who travel the broad highway of life. The language of the "God-Talkers" speaks of continual pursuits, pressing and pushing the Christian's stand on one singular thought, We must, we have to, at all cost get and stay in the presence of The Trinity where Spiritual Kintsukuroi (Kint-ska-roy-e) and Spiritual Kaizen (Kie-zen) will continue to take place.

Before the Christ and being washed in His Blood, the "But as many as receive Him" group was in spiritual darkness, laboring with flawed characters, enslaved by Satan, and walking as dead men. At birth, the disobedience that allowed darkness to invade the blissful life of light and brought the curse of the first Adam marked the souls of humankind. A portrait of imperfection was painted and our futures lay in the balance of eternity. Sin, the transgressor of the law, demanded payment. Justice screamed for the wages to be paid and called for the death of all. The power, clutch, and hold of sin on the children of the first Adam seemed irreversible. Sin was humankind's downfall; it is the wall that keeps humankind from God. Sin is the missing of the mark; it is the perversion, evil disposition, impiety, contempt, and violation of love. The sinfulness of humanity when acknowledged is a remarkable admission. After Christ, we experience spiritual beauty, we become the recipients of God's grace and mercy, lovers of the cross who are blessed and highly favored and walk in the newness of life. Although humankind has the exposure to sin and its environment, it cannot destroy the portrait of influence The Trinity brings into the new life in Christ.

The beauty that comes from the halls of Christendom has a greater effect on the kind of "Ekklesia" you and I will be and become. The acceptance of God's love brings inner beauty as a result of light imposed upon the triune beings inside of "God-Talkers" from the radiance of the throne. Christ's righteousness becomes the Church's righteousness through the work of the Holy Spirit. The darkness of the soul is still present. However, the overshadowing light of Christ imputes power to "God-Talkers" for striking achievement and having abilities as we are ascribing to the "Power to become" and the power to overcome in a devalued world. All things are now possible because of the investment of Heaven's supernatural persuasions.

Inspired by being Kissed by The Trinity the "Power to become" and the power to overcome take on a spirit of gratitude because of a "God-Talkers'" insight. From this insight three important thoughts are revealed:

- The Trinity's "Power to become" and the power to overcome darkness caused by the curse of Adam provide the favor of Christ that is evident in His words and deeds.
- Only what is done in the Name of The Trinity really matters, and only what we do for them will last.
- The Trinity's teaching, comforting, and guiding brings satisfaction and complete rest.

Upon experiencing these important thoughts, the posture of the "Authentic Church" now becomes one of remembrance and reflection. Assuredly, The Trinity's taking care of the "God-Talkers'" natural and spiritual needs is critical. They understand that recipients of the Ultimate Kiss need balm for bruises, joy for sorrow, and peace for chaos. Those who experience the Ultimate Kiss desire growth from the groans of impaired health, opened windows for closed finances, and glue for fractured relationships and disconnected and dysfunctional families. Beneficiaries of the Ultimate Kiss receive grace for thorns, mercy for sins, and faith for doubts. We who pass through death to life encounters want understanding in the midst of confusion, wisdom to practice learned truths, and patience to wait on the Lord. Therefore, following the path of God, growing in the process of God, and accepting the plan of God becomes imperative for "God-Talkers." As we are bedecked and clothed in the likeness of Christ, time brings about its seasons, and wonderful expectations are in the air. Yes, we recall that even after The Fall in the first dispensation, God was still for His people, still coming down to speak with His creation every now and then. Then, in the second dispensation, The Christ came to be with the people from His entrance into the world in the cold animal shed one starry evening until His Ascension from the dusty roads of Galilee into the heavens. And, yes, in the third dispensation, The Holy Spirit is living inside circumcised hearts, minds, and souls. The work of The Trinity's mission is clear: The Trinity will be with Christian "God-Talkers," they will make Christian "God-Talkers," and they will keep their promises to Christian "God-Talkers" by replacing the sinful indebtedness of the first Adam with the royalty, righteousness, glory, and entitlement to life eternal of the second Adam. The gifts of the Ultimate kiss they gave, give, and continue to give are the result of their collective workmanship produced by the redemptive work of Christ's death on the cross.

The Authentic Church avoids erecting the invisible wall that stands between God's House of Prayer and a devalued world. The Authentic Church would never create a barrier that would cause a detriment to those who reside under the snake line.

It is a tragic scene when we see a church that lacks a genuine spirit of Christ and rather than exude God's redemptive power adds to the problems of a devalued world. This renegade or false spirit is apparent by our unwillingness to share the power of the Blood of Christ that can wash away all sin and by our refusal to introduce ourselves to those who are still wrestling with the weight of worldly seduction and have not left their burdens down by the riverside. The church or building or campus that sits on any corner of any street in the universe, masquerading as divinity, separated by an invisible wall from death, and attended by those who do not know the saving grace of Jesus Christ, is not an Authentic Church. True authenticity comes as the Authentic Churches grow inside and outside the four walls. If she (the Authentic Church) refuses to grow and is content with the status quo, she is more of a social club than the House of the Living God. The diminished church, in its lack of divinity, passes death each week and says nothing to those living below the snake line. The Authentic Church seeks to serve themselves and others by speaking out with words that inspire and make known thoughts that the Holy Spirit can dance upon. Then Divinity is moved to tell death that her name has lost its power—with the believer's acceptance of forgiveness, faith, and a friend in Jesus. Those who no longer fear the name of Death should be "servants of the Living God" more commonly called pastor, deacon, or trustee, usher, choir member, or president of the mission society, those who moved from having membership in social clubs to being the real Church that is Christ because of His spilled Blood. Real divinity does not pass Death in silence and allow her to declare, "You deserve to die, go to jail, and lift your eyes from hell." Real divinity doesn't sit next to Death on consecrated pews and ask, "Why are you here, Death? You are not worthy of sitting in the presence of God. Stay on your side of the wall and we will stay on ours." Divinity does not pass Death daily, eyeing a congregation of the hurting and expressing rejection. No, no, divinity speaks to Death and calls forth life in God. Real divinity speaks words that bring life from Death and resurrect new creatures in Christ. Furthermore, the Authentic Church is divinity meeting death, telling of the Ultimate Kiss from The Trinity and the benefits derived from such a Holy Experience. It makes no sense for one piece of dirt attempting to tell another piece of dirt that they are better. But once a piece of dirt has received The Ultimate Kiss it is transformed into modeling clay and able to touch other pieces of dirt that desire to be living, breathing, and part of the growing organism of Trinity.

The God-Talker's Encounter with the Authentic Church
"On the move"

The voices of saints of old have already crossed the River Jordan, but they can still be heard in the present and the future. These voices, which speak to the core of "God-Talkers," are spiritual beings that propel us into different places of spiritual growth and development. As the "But as many as receive Him" group The Trinity gave the "Power to become" and the power to overcome as they move through levels of growth (from glory to glory, from faith to faith) from one court, to the second court, and then on to the third court of Authentic Church.

First, let us clearly define the three courts of authenticity. The *outer court* of the Authentic Church is the approach toward The Trinity. It is here where sinners enter in wanting to be cleansed of sins. Moving on to the *inner court* of the Authentic Church the sinner is rightly positioned to accept The Trinity's invitation to be Kissed by them. Then moving on into the *Holy of Holies* of the Authentic Church is the appeal of The Trinity being answered as their voices beckon us to intentionally move closer to the Throne of Heaven. Moving you and me from one place of spiritual triumph to the next, moving you and me from one spiritual bookmark to the next, marking new insights gained from spiritual failures creates a picturesque view from Heaven of believers striving to become the Authentic Church and operating in a true love connection with The Trinity. It is in this posture of moving you and me to make changes (Spiritual Kaizen) and after these changes (Spiritual Kaizen) that we are led toward constant improvement, constant development, and continuous change for the better.

We become more amenable to these changes as we listen for direction from the voices of The Trinity. There are three voices (although quieted by the first death, as they passed from labor to reward—but not the second death, as they live eternally) that speak to the "God-Talkers" growing in wisdom and stature as they move from one court to the other. Each voice still speaks beyond their graves as the Holy Spirit dances upon their words to be understood and listened to in order to live a life of promise, thanksgiving, and gratitude toward the Ultimate Kisses from The Trinity. For me, they were the voice of my mother, my adopted father, and my best friend. The voice of my mother, "Mae Margret," who said to me on the way to preaching my trial sermon the 4th Sunday of January of 1984, "Gerald, can you sing?" and I replied, "No mama, I cannot sing." Then she said, "Gerald, always remember what is in you will come out of you." Her voice was always spoken with perseverance dancing around her words. Then there was the voice of my adopted father, John H. Rouse, who said to me the 4th Saturday of December of 1984, after he dropped me off at Bennett Hall on the campus of the Interdenominational Theological Center (ITC) in Atlanta Georgia, "Son, dress your mind, heart, and soul with the lessons you will learn as you work toward your Master of Divinity degree." His voice was always spoken with passion dancing upon his words. And the third voice was that of my best friend, E. Thurman Walker, who said to me the 2nd Saturday of May of 1994, upon graduating from United Theological Seminary of Dayton, Ohio, "Let's change our names from Eugene T. Walker to E. Thurman Walker and you change your name from Gerald M. Young to G. Martin Young. Let's highlight our famous middle names, praying God will bless us to make spiritual contributions for the Kingdom like our namesakes, Dr. Howard Thurman and Dr. Martin Luther King, Jr." His voice was always spoken with the pearls of Heaven dancing within his words.

Although from this planet, I still hear his voice every Saturday night, that the time when he'd call telling me to "keep pursuing God, Jesus and the Holy Spirit. No matter how dark the night or how hard the task." I hear him saying, "G. Martin, G. Martin, G Martin, do you remember the time Bishop Bryant preached in chapel in the summer of 1993?" And, I would say, "Yes, I remember the time I almost missed listening to one of the greatest mystic voices of the African Methodist Episcopal Church and beyond." He said, "Do you remember the message?" I would say, "Yes, and I remember going to chapel that day moving through the entrance, then taking my seat on the 33rd pew as Bishop Bryant took his text from Luke 7:37-48. After his introduction I moved to the 23rd pew of the chapel. After his second point I had moved to the 10th pew and when he finished I was standing at the altar crying with my hands raised toward the heavens." Then Thurman would laugh and say to me, "That was the day you moved closer to the flame." I had to agree with "T," I moved closer to The Trinity. For whenever one who has been kissed with Ultimate Kisses over and over again, moving closer and closer to The Trinity, the end result is moving from the outer court to the inner court and into the Holy of Holies! This was my ultimate awesome and longed-for encounter of being loved by The Trinity.

As "God-Talkers" move closer and closer to becoming and being the Authentic Church (individually and corporately) we experience God with more and more power. In that same manner, as the "But as many as receive Him" group submit to the meeting with The Trinity who gives the "Power to become" and the power to overcome the vices of a devalued world, we move closer to having more of the virtues of Heaven. What Bishop Bryant's message did for me, moving me from the 33rd pew to the 23rd pew to the 10th pew and then to the altar of the chapel, is what the Ultimate Kisses of God seeks to do to "God-Talkers." It moves us from the outer court, to the inner court, and into the Holy of Holies of the Authentic Church. With each move of preaching, teaching, worship, stewardship, and fellowship, the Authentic Church (individually and corporately) is moved closer to The Trinity's calling to be and become better than before the meeting. The voice of The Trinity beckons "God-Talkers," bidding us to go down by the riverside, to get into the water, be baptized, be dressed with inner vestments, be a part of The Trinity's general and specific will and make it to the other side of The Jordan.

In so doing, we are also moving through the Five Stages of Growth and Development. Down by the riverside, as I have gleaned over years of trial and error, ups and downs, victories and defeats, faith and failures, and the list goes on and on, are the collective experiences that move us from the courts of The Trinity and are marked by our spiritual growth every step of the way. The "God-Talkers" process of getting to the other side of The Jordan is begun by moving into the court's entrance, similarly as I moved from the 33rd pew to the 23rd pew to the 10th pew and then on to the altar of God. Take note of the process as I see it:

The Outer Court—Where Provincial "God-Talkers" Gather

It begins at the first level with our watching at the riverside with just our feet covered, not wanting to launch out into the deep and allow our full bodies to be underwater. We are satisfied with just being acquainted with The Trinity's goodness, kindness, and inimitable track record. Nonetheless, we still do not want to let go of the world's offerings and make ourselves seemingly content to keep and even glorify those vices that bring empty pleasures. But, The Trinity bids those in the outer courts to come and be a part of the "But as many as receive Him" group and thereby receive the power to become more than one could ever become on their own.

The Inner Court—Where Practical "God-Talkers" Gather

Now the emerging "God-Talkers" come to that juncture in the growth process, the second level where they are wading in the water down by the riverside with the water hitting just to their knees. Now they are thinking we can never look back, lest we be turned into a pillar of salt, as did Lot's wife. "Yet not wanting to go any further" should not their prayer. No, the prayer in this court should be a petition to The Trinity to grow closer to the flame and allow the fire to consume us and use us to be the individual and corporate Authentic Church that is growing, moving from wading in the water to going further in with The Trinity, and looking toward the ultimate mark—the third level. It is here that we have a willingness to go further, do more, exercise more belief and faith, and delve more into the water allowing it to hit us at our waist as the Holy Spirit leads. "But not wanting to go the second mile at the call of God" will not be the prayer that is prayed. No, the prayer that is being prayed as one moves from the proverbial 33rd pew of the inner court to the spiritual goal line of the altar, are shouts of joy and thanksgiving with one's hands raised in Praise because of the spiritual actions of The Trinity. Now, we are moving yet closer to The Trinity as though being drawn by Them to proceed to the fourth level. So we have processed from watching, from wading, to being willing, and now to being "Well-Doers." This is where the water hits in the area of the chest to neck and we begin methodically operating in words and deeds that answer the call of Heaven. We begin going where The Trinity leads and aiding others to come out of the darkened tombs of a devalued world into the light of life that is eternal in the heavens. We have now come from the outer court and into the inner court and are clothed in right minds.

The Holy of Holies—Where Practical, Pastoral, Prophetic, and Professional "God-Talkers" Gather

The categories of growth and development denote the levels of love that are experienced from the Ultimate Kisses of The Trinity. But, let us be clear that it's not a question of what level we are on at this moment. Each level progresses by the Divine timing of The Trinity and with our cooperation. So it is a question of committing to make the move from the outer court into the inner court and then into the Holy of Holies, where ultimately one is under the water and totally sold-out for the Kingdom, the fifth level. Then we see how we process from watching, to wading, to being willing, to be well-doers, and then on to being Worshippers. As Worshippers we are so engrossed in our love for The Trinity that Christians will not rest until we reach the last and the ultimate category of closeness; namely, where we are submerged in our love for the Holy Trinity, eternally grateful for Their giving the Ultimate Kiss to us as we are immersed in their presence, and our heads (logical thinking) go underwater, dying to our former position of standing safely on the riverside! A Hallelujah should go here! We are now at the point of maturing in faith day after day, where the pursuit of spiritual excellence becomes our aim.

It is this fifth level of love that is the consummate desire of The Trinity for us and that invites and empowers us to testify, teach, preach, and let the Authentic Church (individually and corporately) go deeper and deeper into the incalculable Mysteries of The Trinity.

The voices from the past, present, and future speak to encounters with the Authentic Church that is always moving "God-Talkers" closer and closer to the other side of the riverside.

5,000 Men and Women on 500 Corners Encounter the Authentic Church

"The things God cannot do"

Men and women who hear Godly voices of the past, present, and into the future understand the importance of not letting the words of those voices fall on deaf ears, nor allowing powerful words which the Holy Spirit dances upon to move one to empty actions. The Authentic Church cannot simply exist to have Worship, Fellowship, Preaching, Teaching, and Stewardship. She must also have Christian Service and Witnessing! She needs a systematic strategy or strategies to redeem communities from the social ills that are being grappled with and are within the clutches of Satan. The Reverend Jesse Jackson, who once walked with me through the St. Bernard Projects before Katrina hit New Orleans, spoke to persons who were captives to the crack epidemic, and used his voice to declare, "The Authentic Church is here to aid you to become free from the bondage of sin." On the heels of his declaration, multi-talented entertainer Steve Harvey, a professing Christian, was moved to set up mentoring programs in major cities for troubled Black boys, and used his voice and others to tell these young men there is another way.

Journalist Roland Martin, an emerging voice brought to the regular radio listeners of the *Tom Joyner Morning Show*, interviewed Pastor Corey Brooks of Chicago, Illinois. Pastor Brooks leads the congregation of New Beginnings Church and answered the Voice of God to do something positive to combat the ever-present violence that plagues most urban cities. He discussed the plight of urban cities' crime rate and the death of young Black people in the age bracket of 12–25. He said in the interview, "We're off to a great start with 1,300 men that should help impact the city of Chicago. We're trying to build a relationship with young men and establish a rapport." What a model example of Christian Service and Witness from the Authentic Church that leaves the walls of the building to make a difference in this community She is serving! The Church is recruiting 5,000 men to lend their voices and share The Trinity's natural and spiritual actions on 500 corners in Chicago beginning on Fridays starting in June of 2014 through August of 2014. There will also be 5,000 women lending their voices and sharing The Trinity's natural and spiritual actions on 500 corners in Chicago at the same time. This is a strategic move to become the difference in the lives of those who reside below the snake line by having Christian men and Christian women go out to meet and to share with the people on those corners the Ultimate Kiss of The Trinity. They will be testifying to everyone they encounter of the goodness of God and the ten things God can't do. Their testimonies as "God-Talkers" will be enhanced as they endeavor to speak to those above the snake line and those who will become "God-Talkers." The ten things are:

- ***God can't get tired.*** Don't you know anything? Haven't you been listening? God doesn't come and go. God lasts. He's Creator of all you can see or imagine. He doesn't get tired out, doesn't pause to catch his breath. And he knows everything, inside and out. (Isaiah 40:28)
- ***God can't take on a job He can't handle.*** Dear God, my Master, you created earth and sky by your great power—by merely stretching out your arm! There is nothing you can't do. (Jeremiah 32:17)
- ***God can't be unholy.*** Holy, Holy, Holy is God-of-the-Angel-Armies. His bright glory fills the whole earth. (Isaiah 6:3)
- ***God can't be prejudiced.*** Peter fairly exploded with his good news: "It's God's own truth, nothing could be plainer: God plays no favorites! It makes no difference who you are or where you're from—if you want God and are ready to do as he says, the door is open. (Acts 10:34-35)
- ***God can't break a promise.*** Do you think I'd withdraw my holy promise? Or take back words I'd already spoken? (Psalm 89:34)

- ***God can't remember sins he's chosen to forget.*** But I, yes I, am the one who takes care of your sins—that's what I do. I don't keep a list of your sins. (Isaiah 43:25)
- ***God can't make a loser.*** In the Messiah, in Christ, God leads us from place to place in one perpetual victory parade. (2 Corinthians 2:14)
- ***God can't abandon you.*** Be strong. Take courage. Don't be intimidated. Don't give them a second thought because God, your God, is striding ahead of you. He's right there with you. He won't let you down; he won't leave you. (Deuteronomy 31:6)
- ***God can't stop thinking about you.*** Your thoughts—how rare, how beautiful! God, I'll never comprehend them! I couldn't even begin to count them—any more than I could count the sand of the sea. (Psalm 139:17-18)
- ***God can't stop loving you.*** God told them, "I've never quit loving you and never will. Expect love, love, and more love!" (Jeremiah 31:3)

To have these ten things God cannot do as the talking points, the voices of these Godly men and women can share with those on the corners in Chicago The Trinity's invitation that provides reasons to join the "But as many as receive Him" group. This group has great reasons to attend and embrace the meeting down by the riverside. The main reason is that the Holy God who cannot do anything that is not born of love is the same God who can do the impossible over and over again. He keeps on proving Himself to persons who come off the corners and into the "But as many as receive Him" group. This group can stand on the tallest mountain and shout to the top of their voices, "I was homeless but God blessed me with a scholarship to Harvard." David Boone is such a young Black man who is blessed to attend Harvard. And, there's yet another witness who says, "We lived in a homeless shelter with my mom and two siblings and God blessed me with a college scholarship to Georgetown University." Rashema Melson is that young Black woman who is blessed to pursue her studies at Georgetown. There is story after story of the impossible happening around urban America even as the Authentic Church has great, spirit-filled services. However, she too must come down from the mountaintop, spirit-filled services and also take her testimonies of the list of ten things God cannot do to the corners of every corner possible. On those corners could be another David Boone or Rashema Melson. This is exactly the message of this poem that God and I wrote:

> It is good for us to be here to bask in your glory, to
> reflect upon your goodness and rejoice within your story.
> Seeing you from inside out may cause us to wonder.
> Can we stay here out of sight, away from the world and its plunders?
>
> The answer from Jesus is one we'll not soon forget.
> Even Moses and Elias had to have their earthly nests.
> So that we may reach Canaan, He says we must follow
> Heaven's best, for the road less traveled is
> the one that leads to God's divine rest.
> So come off the mountain, but bring the lessons learned.
> The valley keeps calling for answers to life's twists and turns.
>
> Will the church run from quiet hells humankind trod everyday?
> Or will we leave the hallowed hall of God
> Declaring, "He's the only way"?
> The nerve of the Gurus—GodoMubuta, and Lao Tzu.
> To think their words can save people's souls
> And bring their broken hearts through.
> We know not how you feel; yet this one thing we know is true.
>
> Jesus works miracles, signs, and wonders and your
> dark skies then become blue.
> The Trinity gives us power—to follow where They lead.
> Motivated by Their love and music played from David's reed.
> Who would have thought worship could be so
> awesome and so sweet.
> Yes, it's great in Jerusalem, but even better in the streets![2]

Again, we applaud the spirit-filled services at the Ekklesia. They're great! But, afterward The Trinity implores you to take the message to the streets. Voices of the Authentic Church sharing as the salt of the earth and the light on a hill can change the culture in Chicago and beyond with declarations of the natural and spiritual actions of God to young Black persons, young Hispanic persons, young White persons, and all youth regardless of race or ethnicity. Because in every shadow of the steeples across the world are persons who need The Trinity's Kiss and to know the things God cannot do that come with Their caring.

More importantly, let this Ultimate Kiss at least be offered. It's up to those who lurk in the shadows to accept or refuse Heaven's provision and Christ's atonement. The forgiving or pardoning of sin through the death and resurrection of Jesus Christ brings harmony back to the Throne of God and is how abundant life can be achieved. The Authentic Church does not operate under the false illusion that every person who will hear these voices of Godly men and women will accept the atonement of the Christ and come down by the riverside, get into the waters, and press to get to the other side of The Jordan River. Nor is the Authentic Church under the false allusion that this effort of Pastor Brooks and others will stop the violence in the city of Chicago. However, if one life is saved from dying at the hand of senseless killing or if one Black boy, Hispanic boy, White boy, and any boy's destiny is altered to go to college and not to prison, or if one Black girl, Hispanic girl, White girl, and any girl can change her course and direction toward being a "God-Talker" in a positive way, it is worth going to those corners. If some young man or woman will hear and understand the words these "God-Talkers" will give and decide to join the "But as many as receive Him" group, to God Be the Glory. If these young people will submit to meetings with The Trinity who gives the "Power to become" and the power to overcome the vices of a devalued world, they can move closer to having more of the virtues of Heaven. It is worth going the extra mile to exist in this devalued world to reach out to these young people. Dr. Andrew Sung Park from the United Theological Seminary in Dayton, Ohio, said:

As seen in his life, Christ's atoning work was not done as a transaction between God and Satan or between God and Christ, but it was done as the restoration of right relationship between sinners and the sinned-against, through which it bears the fruition of the right relationship between God and humanity. Jesus came to fulfill the original bliss of God's creation so that we may enjoy God's abundant life.[3]

These young men and women Pastor Brooks and other recruits will encounter can be given the voices that lead them out of the shadows of steeples and social ills to the light of The Trinity and to obtaining a life of abundance. They can hear the good news that they can be more than statistics as they are drawn into the river and become those who can swim in the river. Dr. Park continues by saying:

He came for blessings of all creation. The Church needs to see the goal of Jesus' mission in a larger context, to reinterpret it in the public arena, and to pursue it in the public arena.[4]

Dr. Park's words echo divine voices from the past, present, and future that Christian Service and Witnessing has to move from the walls of the church into the public arena. It is apparent Pastor Brooks and his recruits care about what is going on in their communities. And the atonement of Christ is the source of such caring. The "But as many as receive Him" group comes from off corners such as these probably much like Pastor Brooks, the witnessing team, you and me. Someone cared for us enough to go where we were that we too could receive the power to become overcomers—overcomers of corners that are places and spaces of rejection. It is where we were met and where others will be met with the message of the Authentic Church.

What is this message? The message is clearly that what The Trinity cannot do because of its divinity is exactly the very things those who are on those corners really need The Trinity to address. They need the experience of beauty being brought to those corners of ashes, the feel and smell the aroma of the oil of joy for those corners of mourning, and shouts of praise to their corners of fainting.

On Behalf of the Called-Out Ones' Encounter with the Authentic Church
"Our Personal Benefactor"

Imagine The Trinity standing, gazing upon the Ultimate Kissed Authentic Church, and describing in detail the moving metaphors that flow from Their hearts. The "called-out ones" have the highest place in the heart of God and He builds upon and enlarges His praises beyond those given to Her in the past. They are being transformed into the image of His Son. The "called-out ones" were the reason when the Christ looked into the cup and seeing the "But as many as receive Him" group, realizing that only by His death could they have the "Power to become" and the power to overcome, so He marched on to Calvary. Leaving the realm of the Throne He ascended to reside on the inward parts of the "called-out ones," making the difference and influencing virtues and evicting vices. The Trinity gives "called-out ones" the declarations of praise and is gladdened by their heartfelt worship. The Trinity sees spiritual milestone after spiritual milestone testifying of The Trinity's natural and spiritual actions. They gaze at the "called-out ones," happy to see achievements made in Their relationship and partnership with the Ekklesia. The "called-out ones" are beautiful, perfect, and flawless. They are not only the apples of Their eyes; they are captivating in new ways. These God-Talkers are majestic, holy, earnest, and consecrated as never before. Before Them, we are a Church that is pleasing to Their sight. Not just beautiful, but powerful, the result of a progressive union that continues to get closer to Heaven with each breath taken.

We are now in that spiritual place where past struggles have produced a present sanity, and we are serene in our position as the sanctuary of God on earth. Coupled with these truths is the fact that the "called-out ones" are more powerful, magnificent in elevation, exuding with exciting joy, and evoking a sense of wonder and awe.

Yet what makes the "called-out ones" most striking, awe-inspiring, and splendid is the banner or standard of "those who have been called out of the world to go back into the same world telling others of the Good News of Heaven." Impressive is the Authentic Church of God whose conquering troops fly in the wind of God, a banner declaring victory before the enemies of God. Satan and his fallen angels can only look upon the "called-out ones" in jealousy and think of what could have been. God-Talkers have been blessed with victory not because the "called-out ones" desire to be God but because the "called-out ones" desire to be with God. His name causes all the enemies of God to step back and to retreat because of the blood of the Pascal Lamb. The "called-out ones" are an awesome army whose banner each day signals good news. On Sunday, the banner reads "Glory to The Trinity who gives us the victory over Satan, sin, and the grave." On Monday, the banner reads, "Glory to The Trinity who blesses us with the whole armor to fight the good fight." On Tuesday, "Glory to The Trinity whose presence leads us and guides us." On Wednesday it says, "Glory to The Trinity for using us as instruments of His divine love." On Thursday, "Glory to The Trinity for the things He has done." On Friday the banner reads, "Glory to The Trinity that when we are weak, He makes us strong." And, on Saturday, "Glory to The Trinity when we cry unto Him, He hears and answers."

Yes, The Trinity's banner flies over His church, telling the story of victory— how They have blessed us to be more than conquerors. The "called-out ones" are those warriors of the cross who hold up consistently the truth of God— that Jesus reigns. The one who bled, suffered, and died is the Conqueror. The Ekklesia are yet soldiers in His army. Companies of fighters that stand and declare the "called-out ones" are set apart and given victory in His name. God-Talkers are no longer cowards, but heroes, persons who are weak in human flesh yet transformed by the Holy Spirit into saints and slaves freed to become servants that are liberated to tell the world we are both beautiful and conquerors because of our fellowship with the one who overcame—Jesus, the Christ. We are inclined to speak of these great thing while never forgetting what stands between the "called-out ones" and the gathering down by the Riverside. The gaze of the enemy in their endless pursuit to stop the victory march toward the Riverside no longer hinders us.

The sacred and Ultimate Kiss of The Trinity provides much-needed strength. Yet, the forces of evil seek to interrupt the "called-out ones" with the enemies of apathy, folly, and slothfulness. These three deadly traits are the "called-out ones'" worse combatants, and are intended to rob God-Talkers of needed concerns for those residing below the snake line. Their aim is to defuse the morale of "called-out ones," which is required to keep the vision burning bright toward eliminating the Authentic Church's effectiveness to provide the power to become overcomers.

Everyone gets physically tired, spiritually burned out, and mentally exhausted. Working in a devalued world, with persons above and below the snake line, can and will take its toll on any Authentic Church. Since this journey is not a sprint to the finish but a marathon, the "But as many as receive Him" group that The Trinity gave the "Power to become" and the power to overcome must keep putting one foot in front of the other every day, especially in the face of great obstacles and challenges inside and outside the walls of the House of God. Every day renewed strength is required to fight the good fight of faith and stay tapped into the supernatural source of power that the Ultimate Kiss of The Trinity supplies. The inexhaustible supply and power is always available to give the individual in the church as well as the corporate church body the needed natural and spiritual energy to grow and develop into The Trinity's vision. Their vision for the Ekklesia is to keep holding up the blood-stained banner, keep the flame burning, and become the fire by spreading the message of the Gospel into a devalued world, passing out the invitation of John 3:16 on corners of darkness that light can and will shine, realizing that the forces of darkness will not rest and at every turn will seek to drain "the called-out ones" of power to overcome their own flaws and faults. "The Interrogator" who works for Satan will make it dangerous for the "called-out ones" to overcome their fears and failures. The agents of evil operate with the sole intent of making ministry (meeting the needs of ourselves and others) a disastrous undertaking for the "called-out ones" to overcome faithlessness and faithfulness. But the Ultimate Kiss of The Trinity provides deliverance to the "called-out ones" to overcome by giving fortitude and forcefulness. Consider this story from ancient Greece:

> Thousands of years ago in classical Greece, a huge choral and dramatic company practiced endlessly for a huge, important theatrical performance. After they put in a great amount of time, effort, energy, and practice, it was finally time for the show to go on the road.
> But there was one major problem—they ran out of money! These people had given their lives to this production. They had committed all their resources to making sure the performance succeeded. But because they ran out of financing, it meant the show was over—finished! They were washed up before the show ever officially got started. From all appearances, it was the end of the road for them and their dreams. At that exact moment, a wealthy man heard of their crisis, steps into the middle of their situation, and makes a huge financial contribution on behalf of the choir. This contribution "supplied" all they needed to get back in business again! In fact, the gift the man gave was so enormous that it was more than they needed or knew how to spend! This man's contribution was excessively large, abundant, overflowing and overwhelming.[5]

This example of a benefactor's gift was what the choir needed to carry on their performances. In a real sense, a transforming thought and an encouraging word is what the Ultimate Kiss of The Trinity does, not on behalf of the choir, but on behalf of the Authentic Church and all of its members. When she runs out of steam, gets tired from the meeting of needs in her church and community, and doesn't have another ounce of power or resources, The Trinity steps in to be our individual and corporate benefactor, and provides the power to overcome the deadly enemies of apathy, folly, and slothfulness. Like the wealthy man who stepped into our choir story, God-Talkers have experienced time and time again The Trinity stepping in, in the nick of time, supplying much-needed provisions of power, strength, and energy, giving massive, overwhelming, generous contributions of Their presence, power, and dynamic movements of needed help to the "called-out ones." They have more of all the things needed to carry out the vision that has been set before the "But as many as receive Him" group that The Trinity gave the "Power to become" and the power to overcome Satan and his angels' pursuits, more than enough incredible resources and provided strength for the "called-out ones" to gather down by the riverside.

God-Talker's Mission
"Not lying on the Trinity"

The incident went viral and spread across social media like wildfire. It was liked by so many persons because of the inspiration derived from these tragic moments and the messages it sent throughout the Christian Community. The Trinity's presence shines brightest in times of great trials, amidst demonic attacks, and in the face of unprecedented odds against "God-Talkers." The Authentic Church (individual and corporate) saw the news story on TV, and persons posted it on Facebook with millions of Tweets going out all over the globe. A white bus driver from Dayton, Ohio, miraculously escapes from the attack of three Back boys was the storyline. The RTA driver was just driving his route and then it happened, according to the reporter on site that night. On this particular night, there was a gang initiation and within the context of the required shenanigans to be accomplished the gang's target was this bus driver. The story continued by saying this young gang recruit was charged to kill this unarmed White man who was about the business of doing his job to earn a living. Little did they know or realize that this White man was no ordinary man – but a Child of the King, a follower of the Lamb, a water-walker and one empowered by the Holy Ghost. The Inner Immanuel showed strong on this "God-Talker's" behalf. He is always present and ready to move as a representative of the Kingdom. The young gang recruit, according to the report, stabbed the bus driver in the arm with a knife, and shot him in the leg and the other arm. Then he fired two bullets into the man's chest! He thought that this last blow had certainly killed the bus driver. However, it was later determined that the young gang banger was in error in his assumption because the two bullets that went into the chest of the bus driver on arrival encountered the White man's New Testament Bible tucked inside his inner coat pocket! The bullets never reached the target destination or devastation because The Word of God, The Christ, and The Holy Spirit stopped them! A shout goes right here!

But wait, it is later discovered as this White man was telling the officers who arrived on the scene to investigate his claims and speaking to onlookers, that holes began to surface from his account that was given to police. While at the hospital, questions began to surface to the truthfulness of his statements. The officials of RTA and the police launched an investigation. Their findings concluded that the man made up this elaborate lie, extravagant story, and intricate tale. It was all a fabricated incident. As a world shouted at The Trinity's natural and spiritual actions this man's shame is all to be left of his lies. Discredited, disgraced, and discharged by RTA, this man's disheartening story can only change as he experiences deliverance from The Trinity. No reason to lie and say that he was attacked by three young Black men to further add fuel on a generation that really has more scholars than thugs. Surely there was no reason to lie on The Trinity because all that he claimed They have done before over and over again for "God-Talkers" in one way are another. God the Father, God the Son, and God the Holy Spirit do not need anyone lying on what They can do, have done, and will continue to do. The Trinity has defended the helpless, changed the trajectory of Satan's bullets, and shown strong on behalf of the "But as many as received Him" group for eons. Why tell such untruths? Why make up such drama? Why lead people on this merry-go-round of falsehoods?

Here is the deal, I contend, if one claims to be an individual Church member or a part of a corporate Church that believes in The *Insanity of Theology*, being a positive God-Talker and dressed in Inner Vestments, who strives to be and become the Authentic Church, our mission is simple. We cannot LIE on The Trinity like this man!!! *Insanity of Theology* (promotes an ongoing belief and faith in God to turn situations around for the betterment of the individual, the Church, and the community, even when the evidence points to the impossible), a Positive God-Talker (Practical, Pastoral, Prophetic, and Professional), and being dressed with Inner Vestments (God's knowledge, Christ's belief, and the Holy Spirit's empowerment) propel the Authentic Church to walk in Their truth. The truth of the matter is, all They do is give out more Ultimate Kisses and take the "But as many as receive them" group who has been given the "Power to become" and the power to overcome in a devalued world. But to LIE on Their positive actions as did this man is a worthless exercise in the cause of Christ.

We too LIE on The Trinity if the Church makes little effort to be and become the Authentic Church She is called to be in this devalued world.

The mind, heart, and soul must be in constant dialogue and in concert with what one has learned about God, experienced with God, witnessed concerning God, and applied from God's Words in the life of one who champions God. To grapple with one's faith in real-life experiences is where the Insanity of Theology really takes place. In the grappling, the purity of Theology will surface. It is where the discussion of Theological truths by Provincial, Practical, Pastoral, Prophetic, and Professional God-Talkers answer life's most pressing questions and confront life's most critical circumstances that the God-Talker is moved from principles of theology to practices of theology, from ivory tower debates concerning theology to inner triumphs and deliverance that spill over and outward. This spillage outward is the divine nature of God that addresses impossible situations because of theology and mind-blowing treatises dealing with theology to breaking down theology to everyday thoughts and producing coping tools to overcome hurts, harms, and heartaches. Putting on God's knowledge, Christ's belief, The Holy Spirit's empowerment, and the Authentic Church's encounter ensure victory over barrenness, brokenness, and blankness.

Conclusion

It was after 8 a.m. at the kitchen table while eating three eggs sunny side up and drinking some orange juice that I reflected on my wrestling match with "The Interrogator." Some eight or nine years later I thought that my definition of the *Insanity of Theology,* which I gleaned from studying the Gospel of John, was right on point. My definition of theology and my ongoing belief and faith in God to turn situations around for the betterment of the individual, the Church, and the community even when the evidence points to the impossible, has stood up in the face of great trial. It is insane, says "The Interrogator," for people to keep on doing the same thing over and over again with the expectation of a different outcome because of God. Yet for positive God-Talkers everywhere it is a good insanity that brings great results because God is in the equation. The wrestling match has taken on a different tone. The tone of overwhelming confidence has been gleaned, belief that soars above the snake line giving inspiration to those below the snake line has been gained, and faith has won against the odds with all having worked for my good.

In light of my definition of the *Insanity of Theology* that sat in chair number 1, the three burning questions that sat in chair number 2, Dr. Howard Thurman's book *The Creative Encounter* that sat in chair number 3, and my thoughts on Inner Vestments that sat in chair number 4, I have won this match with "The Interrogator" who sat in chair number 5. Because of who sat in the first four chairs the fifth chair participant loses its grip on the outcome of my struggle. I have become stronger, I have become wiser, after the ordeal of being stretched, and I have become better as a result of the fight for those eight or nine years.

It is with that declarations that I encourage you with great authority, in your fights, to remember who sits at the dinner table with you, for you do not sit alone! The participants in the first four chairs at your table are those who bring victory from seemingly win-less skirmishes with "The Interrogator," Satan, and his host of evildoers.

With respect to those five chairs, praises to God that Dr. Jacquelyn Grant's third question posed during my Systematic Theology class, "What does God want displayed in our theological lives?" has been answered. Theology is organic in nature and is constantly growing positive God-Talkers who are on the move toward worshipping from the inside out and wearing Inner Vestments that make the difference for the wearer and those who are not yet properly dressed in a devalued world.

I have learned valuable lessons from putting on the Inner Vestments. I pray you have as well. The Inner Vestment of God's knowledge promotes wisdom in different, challenging situations and instructs the wearer on how to be victorious in those situations. It is the Inner Vestment of belief in Christ that guarantees positive outcomes in the face of insurmountable odds. The Inner Vestment of The Holy Spirit's empowerment is the winning factor against sin and to sinning less. The Inner Vestment of the Authentic Church's encounter makes conquerors for The Trinity's sake in a devalued world. These Inner Vestments have made me more like Christ, more prepared to carry out God's will for my life and more confident to fight the fight of faith.

Grappling with "The Interrogator" will deepen our commitment and resolve to become better in Kingdom building. I claim the victory of having won my nine-year wrestling match. However, I am sure that the "The Interrogator" will come again and again with much stronger assaults against me. He will come against you as well with planned attacks to cripple your commitment and resolve. But, with the *Insanity of Theology* (a good insanity), positive God-Talking, and keeping on Inner Vestments, you and I can win again and again. A shout goes right here!!

Glossary

(Definitions taken from a variety of sources)

Atonement – Describes the saving work that God did through Christ to reconcile the world to himself, and also the state of a person having been reconciled to God. The fact that Jesus Christ died on behalf of all sinners.

Belief – The conviction that God exists and is the Creator and Ruler of all things, the provider and bestowal of eternal salvation through Christ. The strong and welcome conviction or belief that Jesus is the Messiah, through whom we obtain eternal salvation in the Kingdom of God. Having confidence, faith, trust in the triune nature of Almighty God.

Christian Theist – Is likened to a positive "God-Talker." He/she is a fan and follower of the Christ, a believer in the Most High, a walker of faith, a water walker, a witness of God, a Christian (Christ-like), an imitator of Jesus, a sinner saved by grace, a person who has gone by Calvary and received forgiveness of sin and stopped by Pentecost and been endowed with the power to walk right and talk right, a person after God's own heart, a prisoner of hope, an accepter of the Holy Spirit, a claimer of the Body of Christ, one who believes in miracles, signs, and wonders, and one who is a friend of God.

Faith – A conviction or belief respecting man's/woman's relationship to God and divine things, generally with the included idea of trust and holy fervor born of faith and joined with it. It is having confidence and trust in God

Grace – The merciful kindness by which God, exerting his holy influence upon souls, turns them to Christ; keeps, strengthens, and increases them in Christian faith, knowledge, and affection; and kindles them to the exercise of Christian virtues. God giving humankind what is not deserved and giving goodwill and favor.

Heart – The inner man/woman, mind, will, understanding. The center of the total personality, especially with reference to intuition, feeling, or emotion.

Individuation – The transformation one goes through to reach spiritual awareness and become a person of wholeness.

Insanity of Theology – Promotes an ongoing belief and faith in God to turn situations around for the betterment of the individual, the Church, and the community, even when the evidence points to the impossible.

Kaizen – Change that leads toward constant improvement.

Kintsukuroi – Asian term that relates to the "repair of pottery with gold or silver." The process and technique of fixing what has been broken and making it being better than it was before the breaking.

Logos – The essential Word of God, Jesus Christ, the personal wisdom and power in union with God, his minister in creation and government of the universe, the cause of all the world's life, both physical and ethical, which for the procurement of man's salvation put on human nature in the person of Jesus the Messiah, the second person in the Godhead, and shone forth conspicuously from His words and deeds.

Mind – The seat of emotions and passions and the process that reasons, thinks, feels, wills, perceives, and judges.

Nomenclature – A system of names or terms, or the rules for forming these terms in a particular field of arts or sciences.

Snake Line – An invisible, yet very real and definitive line above which humanity seeks to rise above. A level of adversity, a precariously negative existence that diminishes healthy activity and goodness in life. You will never find a snake, nor can a snake breathe, after a certain altitude.

Soul – The uniqueness of the human being derived from the inner being; the breath of humans. The inner being of man/woman. The spiritual part of humans regarded in its moral aspect, or as believed to survive death and be subject to happiness or misery in a life to come.

Spiritual Formation – The growth and development of the whole person by an intentional focus on the spiritual and interior life and Interactions with others in ordinary life. The spiritual practices (prayer, the study of scripture, fasting, simplicity, solitude, confession, worship, etc.).

Theist – The belief in one God as the creator and ruler of the universe, without rejection of revelation.

Theologian – An expert in Theology.

Theology – Beliefs about God, the study of God and the expression of feeling towards God. God-Talk. The field of study and analysis of God and of God's attributes and relations to the universe; the study of divine things or religious truth; divinity.

Triquetra – A three-part interlocking fish symbol that symbolizes the Christian trinity. The word "trinity" comes from the Latin noun "trinitas" meaning "three are one." The Trinity represents the belief that God is one Being made up of three distinct Persons who exist in co-equal, co-eternal communion as the Father, Son, and Holy Spirit.

Triune – Three in one – God the Father, God the Son, and God the Holy Spirit.

Triune – Three parts of man/woman – Mind, heart, and soul.

Truth – What is true in things pertaining to God and humanity with special reference to moral and religious practices.

Notes

Chapter 1 Notes

1 Clanton C.W. Dawson, Jr., "Divine Command Theory," in *An Introduction to Ethics*, ed. Clanton C.W. Dawson, Jr., Louis Colombo, and William Rodriguez (Dubuque, IA: Kendall Hunt, 2014), 1–2.

2 Elaine Pagels, *Beyond Belief: The Secret Gospel of Thomas* (New York: Random House, 2003), 5.

3 Ibid., 6.

4 Tony Evans, *Our God Is Awesome: Encountering the Greatness of Our God* (Chicago, IL: Moody Publishers, 1994), 20.

5 Mervyn A. Warren, *King Came Preaching: The Pulpit Power of Dr. Martin Luther King, Jr.* (Downers Grove, IL: InterVarsity Press 2001), 190.

6 Corrie ten Boom, quoted in the newspaper *Herald of Holiness* (Kansas City, MO: Nazarene Publishing House, 1997), Vol. 86, p. 26.

7 Charles Spurgeon, quoted in J. P. Moreland and William Lane Craig, *Philosophical Foundations for a Christian Worldview* (Downers Grove, IL: InterVarsity Press, 2003), 501.

8 Dietrich Bonhoeffer, *The Cost of Discipleship* (New York: Macmillan Publishing, 1963), 45.

9 Ibid., 47–48.

10 Maya Angelou, "Alone," *The Complete Collected Poems of Maya Angelou* (New York: Random House, 1994), 74.

Chapter 2 Notes

1 Stanley Hauerwas and William H. Willimon, *Resident Aliens: Life in the Christian Colony* (Nashville, TN: Abingdon Press, 1989), preface.

2 Paraphrase of Dr. Cornel West, debate with Molefi Kete Asante at United Theological Seminary, Spring 1993.

3 Mary Stevenson, "Footprints in the Sand," 1936.

4 Martin Bashir, "Clear the Air" segment of the television show *Martin Bashir*. Martin Bashir is a British journalist who was a political commentator for MSNBC. He hosts *Martin Bashir* and is a correspondent for NBC's Dateline NBC.

5 Ibid.

6 Lucy Lind Hogan and Robert Stephen Reid, *The Six Deadly Sins of Preaching: Becoming Responsible for the Faith We Proclaim* (Nashville, TN: Abingdon Press, 2012).

7 Jessica Buchanan and Eric Landemalm, *Impossible Odds: The Kidnapping of Jessica Buchanan and Her Dramatic Rescue by SEAL Team Six* (New York: Atria Books, 2013), 8.

8 Louisa M. R. Stead (1850–1917), "'Tis So Sweet to Trust in Jesus," *African American Heritage Hymnal* (Chicago, IL: GIA Publications, 2001), 68.

Chapter 3 Notes

1 John R. W. Stott, *The Baptism and Fullness of the Holy Spirit* (Downers Grove, IL: InterVarsity Press, 1964), 57.

2 John Owens quote from BrainyQuotes.com.

3 Quotation attributed to *Christian Digest* Magazine, date unknown.

4 William Temple quote from BrainyQuotes.com.

5   The Rev. Canon C. K. Robertson, *A Dangerous Dozen: 12 Christians Who Threatened the Status Quo but Taught Us to Live Like Jesus* (Woodstock, VT: SkyLight Paths Publishing, 2011), x.

6   Ibid., 88.

7   G. Martin Young, *Surviving Category 5 Heartaches: Providing Hope for the Bruised, Battered, and Brokenhearted* (JJG Publishing, 2013), 28.

8   Theodore Roosevelt quote from BrainyQuotes.com.

Chapter 4 Notes

1   http://www.biblestudytools.com/lexicons/greek/nas/ekklesia.html.

2   G. Martin Young, *The Fragrance of Intimacy: A Love Affair Between God and His Church* (JJG Publishing, 2005), 36.

3   Andrew Sung Park, *Triune Atonement: Christ's Healing for Sinners, Victims, and the Whole Creation* (Louisville, KY: Westminster John Knox Press, 2009), xiii.

4   Ibid.

5   Rick Renner, *Sparkling Gems from the Greek: 365 Greek Word Studies for Every Day of the Year to Sharpen Your Understanding of God's Word* (Carol Stream, IL: NavPress, 2003), 4.

About the Author
Dr. G. Martin Young

With an affinity and passion for educational and ecclesiastical excellence, Dr. G. Martin Young has long been visible on the national stage as an advocate for both spiritual and practical application of scripture in the lives of God's people. His pastoral and ministerial experiences include the Longley Baptist Church of Little Rock, Arkansas; the Friendship Baptist Church of Washington, D.C.; and the Tulane Memorial Baptist Church of New Orleans, Louisiana, where he labored as senior pastor/teacher and visionary. Presently, Dr. Young works at the United Theological Seminary in Dayton, Ohio, as a Doctoral of Ministry Mentor/Recruiter.

Dr. Young's other professional ministry affiliations consist of serving as both Dean of Theology and Religious Studies and College Chaplain at the Arkansas Baptist College of Little Rock, Arkansas. He also has served as Interim Dean at Morehouse School of Religion. Dr. Young's educational proving ground encompassed: Southern Illinois University of Edwardsville, Illinois, where he earned a Bachelor of Science degree in Speech Communication; Morehouse School of Religion at the Interdenominational Theological Center of Atlanta, Georgia, where he earned a Master of Divinity degree with specializations in Pastoral Care and Christian Education; and the United Theological Seminary of Dayton, Ohio, where he earned his Doctor of Ministry in Africentric Preaching and Pastoring.

As a Morehouse School of Religion student, Dr. Young was the recipient of the distinguished D. E. King Preaching Award. In 2014 he was inducted into the Morehouse College Preachers Hall of Fame. Dr. Young has penned several literary titles to enrich study practices and encourage readers all across the nation to remain faithful to God. His writings include: *The Religion of the Other Side: The Black Church Called to Evangelize*; *In the Hands of the Savior: Healing Bruised Reeds and Smoking Flax*; *In Search of Rizpah: The Liberated Church Without Walls*; *The Fragrance of Intimacy: A Love Affair Between God and His Church*; *Surviving Category 5 Heartaches: Providing Hope for the Bruised, Battered, and Brokenhearted*; and *Eating and Drinking with the Master: A Fresh Look at the Lord's Supper*. His latest work is *Zechariah's Visions in the Night: The Church Being a Mid-Wife for Prisoners of Hope*.

He is married to Muriel Reine' and is the father of three children: Jouelle, Jillian, and Gerald II.

OTHER PUBLICATIONS BY MMGI BOOKS

Stronger In My Broken Places
By Charles E. Booth

Navigating Pastoral Leadership in the Transition Zone
By D. Darrell Griffin

Standing on Holy Common Ground: An Africentric Ministry Approach to Prophetic Community Engagement
By Lester A. McCorn

The Gospel According to Cancer
By Patricia Gould Champ

These Sisters Can Say It! Volume 1
Edited by Cynthia L. Hale and Darryl D. Sims

These Sisters Can Say It! Volume 2
Edited by Martha Simmons and Darryl D. Sims

Evangelizing and Empowering the Black Male
Edited by Darryl D. Sims

Adam Come Home: Liberating the Minds of Black Men
By Darryl D. Sims

Order your copies today!
Online at mmgibooks.com and at Amazon.com.

For discounts on bulk orders, please call 773.314.7060.